Crisco
COOKIES
for a Year of
CELEBRATIONS

Over 50 Great Cookies from 5 Easy Doughs

Publications International, Ltd.

This edition published by Publications International, Ltd.,
7373 N. Cicero Ave., Lincolnwood, IL 60646.

Recipes from: The Crisco Kitchens

Photography: Proffitt Photography, Chicago

Pictured on the front cover *(clockwise from top left):* Ultimate Chocolate Chip Cookies *(page 12)*, Orange-Glazed Date Nut Bars *(page 26)*, Mocha Chips 'n' Bits *(page 19)*, Frosty's Colorful Cookies *(page 24)*, Cherry Chocolate Chippies *(page 24)*, Pistachio & White Chocolate Cookies *(page 13)*.

Pictured on the back cover *(clockwise from top left):* Aloha Oatmeal Cookies *(page 36)*, Coffee Chip Drops *(page 22)*, Chocolate Cheesecake Bars *(page 84)*, Chewy Brownie Cookies *(page 82)*, Toffee Spattered Sugar Stars *(page 50)*, Pecan Cookies *(page 58)*.

ISBN: 0–7853–1447–4

Manufactured in U.S.A.

8   7   6   5   4   3   2   1

Crisco
COOKIES
for a Year of
CELEBRATIONS

Over 50 Great Cookies from 5 Easy Doughs

INTRODUCTION

Cookies have always been well liked, but every year their popularity seems to grow. Since they are quick to make and easy to transport, cookies fit so easily into today's casual lifestyle. They are as welcome in a child's lunch box as they are at a Fourth-of-July picnic.

Chocolate chip, oatmeal, peanut butter, brownie and sugar cookies are everyone's favorites. The Crisco Kitchens have developed five stellar recipes, one for each of these cookies. In addition to being delicious, these five cookies bake up high and stay soft, moist and chewy—just the way you like them. And these basic recipes are as versatile as they are delectable. Take any one of them, make a few changes and you have a new, exciting and sensational cookie. In fact, there is an entire chapter of great cookies that are easy variations of the basic recipe.

The secret to these moist and chewy cookies is Crisco, the country's leading all-vegetable shortening. Since Crisco never needs refrigeration, there is no need to allow it to soften. It is always ready when you are, so cookies made with Crisco can be baked on the spur of the moment. And now that Crisco Sticks are in supermarkets right next to the familiar blue cans of Crisco and the yellow cans of Butter Flavor Crisco, measuring is as easy as can be. Merely cut the pre-measured foil wrapper for the appropriate amount.

Home bakers can feel confident about using Crisco, since it contains half the saturated fat of butter. (Crisco contains 12 grams of total fat per tablespoon, of which 3 grams are saturated fat, while butter contains 7 grams of saturated fat per tablespoon.)

Some of the mouthwatering cookies on the following pages are pictured in specific holiday settings, but they are not exclusive to those times. While St. Pat's Pinwheels were developed to reflect the green theme of St. Patrick's Day, the peppermint–flavored swirl would be just as enjoyable at Christmas or at a graduation party. So use your imagination and enjoy these cookies all year round. Let the versatility of these five cookie recipes make any get-together a special occasion.

TIPS FOR BAKING GREAT COOKIES EVERY TIME

General Guidelines

• Read the entire recipe before you begin to make sure you have all the ingredients and baking utensils.

• Prepare baking pans and baking sheets according to recipe directions. Grease pans with Crisco only when greasing is called for in directions. Adjust oven racks and preheat the oven.

• Measure all ingredients accurately.

• Follow the recipe directions and baking times exactly. Check for doneness at the minimum baking time using the test given in the recipe.

Measuring

• Use standardized dry measuring cups for all dry ingredients and ingredients such as Crisco, peanut butter, nuts, dried fruit, coconut, fresh fruit, jams and jellies.

• Spoon flour into the correct measuring cup to overflowing and level it off with the straight edge of a metal spatula. Do not dip the measuring cup into the flour or tap the measuring cup on the counter as this will pack the flour.

• Press brown sugar into the correct measuring cup, fill to overflowing and level it off with a straight edge. It should hold the shape of the cup when turned out.

• Press Crisco or Butter Flavor Crisco into the correct measuring cup. Cut through with a knife or spatula and press again to eliminate air pockets. Level it off with a straight edge.

• Use standardized glass or clear plastic liquid measuring cups with a pouring spout to measure all liquid ingredients. Place the cup on a level surface, fill to the desired mark and check the measurement at eye level.

• Use standardized graduated measuring spoons, not eating or serving spoons, for measuring small amounts of ingredients. For dry ingredients, fill the spoon to overflowing and level it off with a straight edge.

Mixing

• Beat Crisco, sugar and other ingredients according to the recipe directions for several minutes to insure proper creaming.

• Sifting of flour is not necessary. Stir together the flour, baking soda, salt and spices before adding to the shortening mixture. Larger amounts of flour should be added gradually to the shortening mixture.

• Do not overmix the dough as this will toughen cookies. If using a hand mixer, it may be necessary to stir in the last portion of flour with a wooden spoon.

• Stir in chips, raisins, nuts and fruit with a wooden spoon.

Baking

• Use sturdy baking sheets with little or no sides. Allow 1 inch of space between the baking sheet and the sides of the oven. This allows heat to circulate in the oven during baking and promotes even browning. Cookies baked on insulated baking sheets may need 1 to 2 minutes longer baking time.

• Bake only one baking sheet at a time in the center of the oven. If cookies brown unevenly, rotate the baking sheet from front to back halfway through the baking time. If you do use more than one baking sheet at a time, rotate the sheets from the top rack to the bottom rack halfway through baking time. Space oven racks 6 inches apart. Allow the baking sheets to cool between batches. Dough will spread if placed on a hot baking sheet.

• Watch cookies carefully during baking to avoid overbaking. Follow the recipe for yield and size since baking time is determined for that size cookie.

• Allow cookies to remain on baking sheets for 2 minutes before removing to sheets of foil, unless otherwise stated. Cool cookies completely before storing.

Problem Solving

• Cookies are dry: This is usually the result of using too much flour or too little liquid. Always measure ingredients accurately.

• Cookies are too brown: If only the bottoms are too brown, the baking sheet may be too close to the bottom of the oven.

Move the rack to a higher position. If both the tops and bottoms of cookies are too brown, either the oven is too hot or there is insufficient air circulation around the baking sheet. Check the oven temperature with an oven thermometer or use a smaller baking sheet. Another cause of overbrowning is overbaking. Check cookies for doneness at the minimum baking time.

• Cookies spread too much or spread into each other: One of the most common causes for cookies spreading too much is using too little flour or too much liquid. Placing cookie dough on hot baking sheets or making cookies too large are other possible causes. Always cool baking sheets to room temperature before reusing and follow recipe directions and yield for proper-sized cookies. If cookies are the correct size but still spread into each other, the portioned dough may have been placed too close together on the baking sheet.

Storage

• Store cooled cookies at room temperature in airtight containers. Store each kind separately to prevent transfer of flavor and changes in texture. Freeze baked cookies in airtight containers or freezer bags for up to six months.

TIPS ON PACKING COOKIES FOR MAILING

• Wrap large, delicate or decorated cookies individually in plastic wrap. Pack cookies in an airtight container. Place heavier cookies at the bottom of the container or pack them in a separate container.

• Place the container in a larger box. Cushion with crumpled newspaper, styrofoam or air–popped popcorn. For a more festive look, wrap the container in gift paper and cushion with crumpled colored tissue paper or metallic tinsel.

• Bar cookies can be baked in disposable aluminum foil pans. When cool, cover pans with foil and pack the pans in a box. Cushion with crumpled newspaper.

• Seal outer box with packing tape.

ULTIMATE CHOCOLATE CHIP COOKIES

Luscious morsels of chocolate and perhaps some crunchy pecans nestled in a soft chewy cookie richly flavored with brown sugar and vanilla—these are the qualities you'll find in Crisco's Ultimate Chocolate Chip Cookies. And, as you will see on the pages that follow, this all-time family favorite recipe can be dressed up for special occasions and the familiar flavors of chocolate and pecans can be traded for a variety of different tastes.

This taste-tempting recipe can be easily varied to create cookies that bear no resemblance to a traditional chocolate chip cookie. Lemonade Cookies with their refreshing citrus flavor are just right for a bridal shower and Maple Walnut Cookies will become a much loved late-night snack. Captivate the kids with Peanut Butter Treats by simply substituting quartered miniature peanut butter cups for the chocolate chips and pecans.

In this chapter are ideas for festive Christmas cookies, such as Cherry Chocolate Chippies and Frosty's Colorful Cookies. Coffee Chip Drops are perfect for your Valentine's Day sweetheart and Pecan Pralines with bits of caramelized sugar and pecans are a perfect addition to any springtime celebration. Whatever variations you choose to bake, the results will delight everyone!

Ultimate Chocolate Chip Cookies
(page 12)

Ultimate Chocolate Chip Cookies

1¼ cups firmly packed light
    brown sugar
¾ cup Butter Flavor Crisco
    all-vegetable shortening
    or ¾ Butter Flavor
    Crisco Stick
2 tablespoons milk
1 tablespoon vanilla

1 egg
1¾ cups all-purpose flour
1 teaspoon salt
¾ teaspoon baking soda
1 cup (6 ounces) semisweet
    chocolate chips
1 cup coarsely chopped
    pecans* (optional)

*If pecans are omitted, add an additional ½ cup semisweet chocolate chips.

1. Heat oven to 375°F. Place sheets of foil on countertop for cooling cookies.

2. Place brown sugar, shortening, milk and vanilla in large bowl. Beat at medium speed of electric mixer until well blended. Add egg; beat well.

3. Combine flour, salt and baking soda. Add to shortening mixture; beat at low speed just until blended. Stir in chocolate chips and pecans, if desired.

4. Drop dough by rounded measuring tablespoonfuls 3 inches apart onto ungreased baking sheets.

5. Bake one baking sheet at a time at 375°F for 8 to 10 minutes for chewy cookies, or 11 to 13 minutes for crisp cookies. *Do not overbake.* Cool 2 minutes on baking sheet. Remove cookies to foil to cool completely.
Makes about 3 dozen cookies

Pistachio and White Chocolate Cookies

1 cup shelled pistachio nuts
1¼ cups firmly packed light brown
    sugar
¾ cup Butter Flavor Crisco
    all-vegetable shortening or ¾
    Butter Flavor Crisco Stick
2 tablespoons milk
1 tablespoon vanilla
1 egg
1¾ cups all-purpose flour
1 teaspoon salt
¾ teaspoon baking soda
1 cup white chocolate chips or chunks

1. Heat oven to 350°F. Spread pistachio nuts on baking sheet. Bake at 350°F for 7 to 10 minutes or until toasted, stirring several times. Place nuts in kitchen towel; rub with towel to remove most of skin. Cool nuts. Chop coarsely; reserve.

2. *Increase oven temperature to 375°F.* Place sheets of foil on countertop for cooling cookies.

3. Place brown sugar, shortening, milk and vanilla in large bowl. Beat at medium speed of electric mixer until well blended. Add egg; beat well.

4. Combine flour, salt and baking soda. Add to shortening mixture; beat at low speed just until blended. Stir in white chocolate chips and reserved pistachios.

5. Drop dough by rounded measuring tablespoonfuls 3 inches apart onto ungreased baking sheets.

6. Bake one baking sheet at a time at 375°F for 8 to 10 minutes for chewy cookies, or 11 to 13 minutes for crisp cookies. *Do not overbake.* Cool 2 minutes on baking sheet. Remove cookies to foil to cool completely.
        Makes about 3 dozen cookies

For a festive Christmas buffet table, tie the silverware and napkins with brightly colored ribbons, tucking in sprigs of evergreen for an aromatic touch. Or try stuffing silverware into small, inexpensive stockings along with tiny gaily wrapped gifts for each guest.

Maple Walnut Cookies

1¼ cups firmly packed light
    brown sugar
¾ cup Butter Flavor Crisco
    all-vegetable shortening
    or ¾ Butter Flavor
    Crisco Stick
2 tablespoons maple syrup
1 teaspoon vanilla

1 teaspoon maple extract
1 egg
1¾ cups all-purpose flour
1 teaspoon salt
¾ teaspoon baking soda
½ teaspoon cinnamon
1½ cups chopped walnuts
30 to 40 walnut halves

1. Heat oven to 375°F. Place sheets of foil on countertop for cooling cookies.

2. Place brown sugar, shortening, maple syrup, vanilla and maple extract in large bowl. Beat at medium speed of electric mixer until well blended. Add egg; beat well.

3. Combine flour, salt, baking soda and cinnamon. Add to shortening mixture; beat at low speed just until blended. Stir in chopped walnuts.

4. Drop dough by rounded measuring tablespoonfuls 3 inches apart onto ungreased baking sheets. Press walnut half into center of each cookie.

5. Bake one baking sheet at a time at 375°F for 8 to 10 minutes for chewy cookies, or 11 to 13 minutes for crisp cookies. *Do not overbake.* Cool 2 minutes on baking sheet. Remove cookies to foil to cool completely.   *Makes about 3 dozen cookies*

*Top to bottom: Maple Walnut
Cookies, Peanut Butter Treats
(page 25)*

Lemonade Cookies

Need an idea for a party that will appeal to both children and adults? Plan an ice cream party—it's sure to please everyone. Set a buffet table with several flavors of ice cream or frozen yogurt, allowing at least two medium scoops per person. (One quart will yield about eight medium scoops of ice cream.) Provide a variety of sundae toppers — ice cream toppings, fruits, nuts and candies. Broken cookies, such as Peanut Butter Treats (page 25) and Chewy Brownie Cookies (page 82), make great toppers. And be sure to include these citrus-flavored Lemonade Cookies as a delicious accompaniment.

1¼ cups granulated sugar
¾ cup Butter Flavor Crisco
    all-vegetable shortening
    or ¾ Butter Flavor Crisco Stick
2 tablespoons freshly squeezed lemon
    juice
1 tablespoon grated lemon peel
1 teaspoon vanilla
1 teaspoon lemon extract
1 egg
1¾ cups all-purpose flour
¾ teaspoon baking soda
½ teaspoon salt
½ cup flaked coconut (optional)

1. Heat oven to 375°F. Place sheets of foil on countertop for cooling cookies.

2. Place sugar, shortening, lemon juice, lemon peel, vanilla and lemon extract in large bowl. Beat at medium speed of electric mixer until well blended. Add egg; beat well.

3. Combine flour, baking soda and salt. Add to shortening mixture; beat at low speed just until blended.

4. Drop dough by rounded measuring tablespoonfuls 3 inches apart onto ungreased baking sheets. Sprinkle tops with coconut, if desired.

5. Bake one baking sheet at a time at 375°F for 8 to 10 minutes or until cookies are set and edges are lightly browned. (Watch closely; do not allow coconut to burn.) *Do not overbake.* Cool 2 minutes on baking sheet. Remove cookies to foil to cool completely.   *Makes about 3 dozen cookies*

Top to bottom: Chocolate Chip Ice Cream Sandwiches (page 18), Lemonade Cookies

Chocolate Chip Ice Cream Sandwiches

1¼ cups firmly packed light brown sugar
¾ cup Butter Flavor Crisco all-vegetable shortening or ¾ Butter Flavor Crisco Stick
2 tablespoons milk
1 tablespoon vanilla

1 egg
1¾ cups all-purpose flour
1 teaspoon salt
¾ teaspoon baking soda
1 cup semisweet chocolate chips
1 cup chopped pecans
2 pints ice cream, any flavor

1. Heat oven to 375°F. Place sheets of foil on countertop for cooling cookies.

2. Place brown sugar, shortening, milk and vanilla in large bowl. Beat at medium speed of electric mixer until well blended. Add egg; beat well.

3. Combine flour, salt and baking soda. Add to shortening mixture; beat at low speed just until blended. Stir in chocolate chips and pecans.

4. Measure ¼ cup dough; shape into ball. Repeat with remaining dough. Place balls 4 inches apart on ungreased baking sheets. Flatten balls into 3-inch circles.

5. Bake one baking sheet at a time at 375°F for 10 to 12 minutes or until cookies are lightly browned. *Do not overbake.* Cool 2 minutes on baking sheet. Remove cookies to foil to cool completely.

6. Remove ice cream from freezer to soften slightly. Measure ½ cup ice cream; spread onto bottom of one cookie. Cover with flat side of second cookie. Wrap sandwich in plastic wrap. Place in freezer. Repeat with remaining cookies and ice cream.

Makes about 10 ice cream sandwiches

Note: Chocolate Chip Ice Cream Sandwiches should be eaten within two days. After two days, cookies will absorb moisture and become soggy. If longer storage is needed, make and freeze cookies, but assemble ice cream sandwiches within two days of serving.

Mocha Chips 'n' Bits

Cookies

1¼ cups firmly packed light brown sugar

¾ cup Butter Flavor Crisco all-vegetable shortening or ¾ Butter Flavor Crisco Stick

2 tablespoons milk

1 tablespoon instant coffee powder

1 tablespoon vanilla

1 egg

1¾ cups all-purpose flour

1½ tablespoons unsweetened cocoa powder

1 teaspoon salt

¾ teaspoon baking soda

1 cup (6 ounces) milk chocolate chips

1 cup coarsely chopped pecans

4 ounces bittersweet chocolate, cut into chunks

Icing

1 cup white chocolate chips

1 teaspoon Crisco all-vegetable shortening

1. Heat oven to 375°F. Place sheets of foil on countertop for cooling cookies.

2. Place brown sugar, shortening, milk, instant coffee and vanilla in large bowl. Beat at medium speed of electric mixer until well blended. Add egg; beat well.

3. Combine flour, cocoa, salt and baking soda. Add to shortening mixture; beat at low speed just until blended. Stir in chocolate chips, pecans and chocolate chunks.

4. Drop dough by rounded measuring tablespoonfuls 3 inches apart onto ungreased baking sheets.

5. Bake one baking sheet at a time at 375°F for 8 to 10 minutes for chewy cookies, or 11 to 13 minutes for crisp cookies. *Do not overbake.* Cool 2 minutes on baking sheet. Remove cookies to foil to cool completely.

6. For icing, place white chocolate chips and shortening in heavy, resealable sandwich bag; seal bag. Microwave at 50% (MEDIUM) for 1 minute. Knead bag. If necessary, microwave at 50% for another 30 seconds at a time until mixture is smooth when kneaded. Cut small tip off corner of bag. Pipe shapes on cookies or drizzle randomly.

Makes about 3 dozen cookies

Note: White chocolate chips and shortening can be melted by placing resealable bag in bowl of hot water.

Chocolate Chip Cookie Bars

1¼ cups firmly packed light brown
    sugar
¾ cup Butter Flavor Crisco
    all-vegetable shortening or ¾
    Butter Flavor Crisco Stick
2 tablespoons milk
1 tablespoon vanilla
1 egg
1¾ cups all-purpose flour
1 teaspoon salt
¾ teaspoon baking soda
1 cup (6 ounces) semisweet chocolate
    chips
1 cup coarsely chopped pecans*
    (optional)

*If pecans are omitted, add an additional
½ cup semisweet chocolate chips.

1. Heat oven to 350°F. Grease 13 × 9-inch
baking pan. Place cooling rack on
countertop.

2. Place brown sugar, shortening, milk and
vanilla in large bowl. Beat at medium speed
of electric mixer until well blended. Add
egg; beat well.

3. Combine flour, salt and baking soda. Add
to shortening mixture; beat at low speed just
until blended. Stir in chocolate chips and
pecans, if desired.

4. Press dough evenly onto bottom of
prepared pan.

5. Bake at 350°F for 20 to 25 minutes or
until lightly browned and firm in the center.
Do not overbake. Cool completely on cooling
rack. Cut into 2 × 1½-inch bars.
Makes about 3 dozen bars

*Bar cookies are done
when the center is
firm to the touch or
a wooden pick
inserted in the
center comes out
clean.*

*The best way to store
bar cookies is right
in the pan in which
they were baked.
Cover tightly with
plastic wrap or
aluminum foil.*

Chocolate Chip Cookie Bars

Coffee Chip Drops

Chocolate kiss candies atop these coffee-flavored cookies send a loving message to your sweetheart on Valentine's Day.

1¼ cups firmly packed light brown
    sugar
¾ cup Butter Flavor Crisco
    all-vegetable shortening
    or ¾ Butter Flavor Crisco Stick
2 tablespoons cold coffee
1 teaspoon vanilla
1 egg
1¾ cups all-purpose flour
1 tablespoon finely ground French
    roast or espresso coffee beans
1 teaspoon salt
¾ teaspoon baking soda
½ cup semisweet chocolate chips
½ cup milk chocolate chips
½ cup coarsely chopped walnuts
30 to 40 chocolate kiss candies,
    unwrapped

1. Heat oven to 375°F. Place sheets of foil on countertop for cooling cookies.

2. Place brown sugar, shortening, coffee and vanilla in large bowl. Beat at medium speed of electric mixer until well blended. Add egg; beat well.

3. Combine flour, ground coffee, salt and baking soda. Add to shortening mixture; beat at low speed just until blended. Stir in chocolate chips and walnuts.

4. Drop dough by rounded measuring tablespoonfuls 2 inches apart onto ungreased baking sheets.

5. Bake one baking sheet at a time at 375°F for 8 to 10 minutes or until cookies are lightly browned and just set. *Do not overbake.* Place 1 candy in center of each cookie. Cool 2 minutes on baking sheet. Remove cookies to foil to cool completely.
Makes about 3 dozen cookies

Top to bottom: Coffee Chip Drops,
Chocolate Cheesecake Bars (page 84)

Frosty's Colorful Cookies

1¼ cups firmly packed light
    brown sugar
¾ cup Butter Flavor Crisco
    all-vegetable shortening
    or ¾ Butter Flavor
    Crisco Stick
2 tablespoons milk

1 tablespoon vanilla
1 egg
1¾ cups all-purpose flour
1 teaspoon salt
¾ teaspoon baking soda
2 cups red and green candy-
    coated chocolate pieces

1. Heat oven to 375°F. Place sheets of foil on countertop for cooling cookies.

2. Place brown sugar, shortening, milk and vanilla in large bowl. Beat at medium speed of electric mixer until well blended. Add egg; beat well.

3. Combine flour, salt and baking soda. Add to shortening mixture; beat at low speed just until blended. Stir in candy-coated chocolate pieces.

4. Drop dough by rounded measuring tablespoonfuls 3 inches apart onto ungreased baking sheets.

5. Bake one baking sheet at a time at 375°F for 8 to 10 minutes for chewy cookies, or 11 to 13 minutes for crisp cookies. *Do not overbake.* Cool 2 minutes on baking sheet. Remove cookies to foil to cool completely. *Makes about 3 dozen cookies*

Cherry Chocolate Chippies

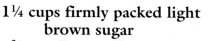

1¼ cups firmly packed light
    brown sugar
¾ cup Butter Flavor Crisco
    all-vegetable shortening
    or ¾ Butter Flavor
    Crisco Stick
1 teaspoon vanilla
1 teaspoon almond extract
1 egg

1¾ cups all-purpose flour
1 teaspoon salt
¾ teaspoon baking soda
1 cup (6 ounces) semisweet
    chocolate chips
1 cup well-drained
    maraschino cherries,
    coarsely chopped

1. Heat oven to 375°F. Place sheets of foil on countertop for cooling cookies.

2. Place brown sugar, shortening, vanilla and almond extract in large bowl. Beat at medium speed of electric mixer until well blended. Add egg; beat well.

3. Combine flour, salt and baking soda. Add to shortening mixture; beat at low speed just until blended. Stir in chocolate chips and cherries.

4. Drop dough by rounded measuring tablespoonfuls 2 inches apart onto ungreased baking sheets.

5. Bake one baking sheet at a time at 375°F for 8 to 10 minutes for chewy cookies, or 11 to 13 minutes for crisp cookies. *Do not overbake.* Cool 2 minutes on baking sheet. Remove cookies to foil to cool completely.   *Makes about 3 dozen cookies*

Peanut Butter Treats

1¼ cups firmly packed light
    brown sugar
¾ cup Butter Flavor Crisco
    all-vegetable shortening
    or ¾ Butter Flavor
    Crisco Stick
2 tablespoons milk
1 tablespoon vanilla
1 egg

1¾ cups all-purpose flour
1 teaspoon salt
¾ teaspoon baking soda
2 cups (about 32) miniature
    peanut butter cups,
    unwrapped and
    quartered or coarsely
    chopped

1. Heat oven to 375°F. Place sheets of foil on countertop for cooling cookies.

2. Place brown sugar, shortening, milk and vanilla in large bowl. Beat at medium speed of electric mixer until well blended. Add egg; beat well.

3. Combine flour, salt and baking soda. Add to shortening mixture; beat at low speed just until blended. Stir in peanut butter cup quarters.

4. Drop dough by rounded measuring tablespoonfuls 3 inches apart onto ungreased baking sheets.

5. Bake one baking sheet at a time at 375°F for 8 to 10 minutes or until cookies are lightly browned. *Do not overbake.* Cool 2 minutes on baking sheet. Remove cookies to foil to cool completely.
                                    Makes about 3 dozen cookies

Orange-Glazed Date Nut Bars

Christmas is a great time for entertaining friends and family, but sometimes it's difficult to coordinate everyone's busy schedules. Why not plan an open house that will allow guests to stop in during their busy day? Set a buffet table with make-your-own sandwiches for early afternoon and prepare a large pot of spicy chili or hearty soup for evening. No matter what the menu, an assortment of make-ahead holiday cookies will be welcomed by all your guests.

Cookie Base
1¼ cups firmly packed light brown sugar
¾ cup Butter Flavor Crisco all-vegetable shortening or ¾ Butter Flavor Crisco Stick
2 tablespoons orange juice
1 tablespoon vanilla
1 tablespoon grated orange peel
1 egg
1¾ cups all-purpose flour
1 teaspoon salt
¾ teaspoon baking soda
1 cup chopped dates
1 cup chopped walnuts

Glaze
1½ cups confectioners sugar
2 tablespoons orange juice

1. Heat oven to 350°F. Grease 13 × 9-inch baking pan. Place cooling rack on counter.

2. Place brown sugar, shortening, orange juice, vanilla and orange peel in large bowl. Beat at medium speed of electric mixer until well blended. Add egg; beat well.

3. Combine flour, salt and baking soda. Add to shortening mixture; beat at low speed just until blended. Stir in dates and walnuts.

4. Press dough into prepared pan.

5. Bake at 350°F for 20 to 25 minutes or until lightly browned and firm. *Do not overbake.* Cool completely on cooling rack.

6. For glaze, combine confectioners sugar and orange juice. Stir until smooth. Spread glaze over cookie base. Cut into 2 × 1½-inch bars. Garnish if desired.

Makes 3 dozen bars

Top to bottom: Raspberry Linzer Rounds (page 61), Orange-Glazed Date Nut Bars

Pecan Praline Cookies

Praline
1½ cups chopped pecans
½ cup granulated sugar
3 tablespoons water

Cookies
1¼ cups firmly packed light
    brown sugar
¾ cup Butter Flavor Crisco
    all-vegetable shortening
    or ¾ Butter Flavor
    Crisco Stick

2 tablespoons milk
1 tablespoon vanilla
1 egg
1¾ cups all-purpose flour
1 teaspoon salt
¾ teaspoon baking soda

1. Heat oven to 375°F. Place sheets of foil on countertop for cooling cookies.

2. For praline, spread pecans on baking sheet; bake at 375°F for 10 minutes or until lightly toasted, stirring several times. Reserve pecans. Grease baking sheet.

3. Place granulated sugar and water in small saucepan. Bring to boil, stirring occasionally. Cover; boil 2 minutes. Uncover; cook 2 minutes or until mixture becomes golden brown in color. Add reserved pecans; stir until evenly coated. Spread on prepared baking sheet. Cool completely. Place hardened praline in heavy resealable plastic bag; seal. Crush with bottom of small heavy skillet until pieces are small.

4. For cookies, place brown sugar, shortening, milk and vanilla in large bowl. Beat at medium speed of electric mixer until well blended. Add egg; beat well.

5. Combine flour, salt and baking soda. Add to shortening mixture; beat at low speed just until blended. Stir in 1½ cups of crushed praline.

6. Shape dough into 1-inch balls. Dip top of each ball into remaining crushed praline. Place 3 inches apart on ungreased baking sheets.

7. Bake one baking sheet at a time at 375°F for 9 to 11 minutes or until cookies are lightly browned. *Do not overbake.* Cool 2 minutes on baking sheet. Remove cookies to foil to cool completely.

Makes about 3 dozen cookies

Pecan Praline Cookies

CHEWY OATMEAL COOKIES

Dotted with plump raisins and scented with cinnamon, classic oatmeal cookies have been around for most of the 20th century and had changed very little until the Crisco Kitchens developed the Chewy Oatmeal Cookie. What makes these so special is all there in the name—they are chewy and soft, so the nutty flavor and rich texture of the oatmeal does not leave a dry feel in the mouth.

The Crisco Kitchens have also found that Chewy Oatmeal Cookies are extremely versatile. Just by changing a few ingredients in this recipe, you can make a delightful array of new cookies all uniquely different from the basic recipe. Replace the raisins with pineapple and coconut and enjoy Aloha Oatmeal Cookies. Add grated carrots and chopped apple and discover Good 'n' Tasties. The variations are not limited to just drop cookies. This easy-to-make dough with a few simple changes can be pressed into a baking pan for the base of fabulous treats, such as Oatmeal Praline Cheese Bars and Peach Oatmeal Bars.

For those who think that a cookie isn't a cookie without a sweet-flavored chip, this chapter includes recipes with bits of chocolate and toffee. And like every other recipe in this chapter, they begin with the same easy basic recipe.

Chewy Oatmeal Cookies (page 32)

Chewy Oatmeal Cookies

1¼ cups firmly packed light
    brown sugar
¾ cup Butter Flavor Crisco
    all-vegetable shortening
    or ¾ Butter Flavor
    Crisco Stick
1 egg
⅓ cup milk
1½ teaspoons vanilla

3 cups quick oats, uncooked
1 cup all-purpose flour
½ teaspoon baking soda
½ teaspoon salt
¼ teaspoon cinnamon
1 cup raisins
1 cup coarsely chopped
    walnuts

1. Heat oven to 375°F. Grease baking sheets. Place sheets of foil on countertop for cooling cookies.

2. Place brown sugar, shortening, egg, milk and vanilla in large bowl. Beat at medium speed of electric mixer until well blended.

3. Combine oats, flour, baking soda, salt and cinnamon. Add to shortening mixture; beat at low speed just until blended. Stir in raisins and walnuts.

4. Drop dough by rounded measuring tablespoonfuls 2 inches apart onto prepared baking sheets.

5. Bake one baking sheet at a time at 375°F for 10 to 12 minutes or until cookies are lightly browned. *Do not overbake.* Cool 2 minutes on baking sheet. Remove cookies to foil to cool completely.

Makes about 2½ dozen cookies

Fall Harvest Oatmeal Cookies

1¼ cups firmly packed light
    brown sugar
¾ cup Butter Flavor Crisco
    all-vegetable shortening
    or ¾ Butter Flavor
    Crisco Stick
1 egg
⅓ cup milk
1 tablespoon grated orange
    peel
1½ teaspoons vanilla
3 cups quick oats, uncooked

1 cup all-purpose
    flour
1½ teaspoons cinnamon
½ teaspoon baking soda
½ teaspoon salt
¼ teaspoon nutmeg
¼ teaspoon ground cloves
1 cup coarsely chopped,
    peeled apples
1 cup raisins
1 cup coarsely chopped
    walnuts

1. Heat oven to 375°F. Grease baking sheets. Place sheets of foil on countertop for cooling cookies.

2. Place brown sugar, shortening, egg, milk, orange peel and vanilla in large bowl. Beat at medium speed of electric mixer until well blended.

3. Combine oats, flour, cinnamon, baking soda, salt, nutmeg and cloves. Add to shortening mixture; beat at low speed just until blended. Stir in apples, raisins and walnuts.

4. Drop dough by rounded measuring tablespoonfuls 2 inches apart onto prepared baking sheets.

5. Bake one baking sheet at a time at 375°F for 10 to 12 minutes or until cookies are lightly browned. *Do not overbake.* Cool 2 minutes on baking sheet. Remove cookies to foil to cool completely.

Makes about 2½ dozen cookies

Cranberry Nut Oatmeal Cookies

1¼ cups firmly packed light brown sugar
¾ cup Butter Flavor Crisco all-vegetable shortening or ¾ Butter Flavor Crisco Stick
1 egg
⅓ cup milk
1½ teaspoons vanilla
1 teaspoon grated orange peel
3 cups quick oats, uncooked
1 cup all-purpose flour
½ teaspoon baking soda
½ teaspoon salt
¼ teaspoon cinnamon
1 cup dried cranberries
1 cup coarsely chopped walnuts

1. Heat oven to 375°F. Grease baking sheets. Place sheets of foil on countertop for cooling cookies.

2. Place brown sugar, shortening, egg, milk, vanilla and orange peel in large bowl. Beat at medium speed of electric mixer until well blended.

3. Combine oats, flour, baking soda, salt and cinnamon. Add to shortening mixture; beat at low speed just until blended. Stir in cranberries and walnuts.

4. Drop dough by rounded measuring tablespoonfuls 2 inches apart onto prepared baking sheets.

5. Bake one baking sheet at a time at 375°F for 10 to 12 minutes or until cookies are lightly browned. *Do not overbake.* Cool 2 minutes on baking sheet. Remove cookies to foil to cool completely.
                    Makes about 2½ dozen cookies

Top to Bottom: Fall Harvest Oatmeal Cookies (page 33), Cranberry Nut Oatmeal Cookies

While cookies may not be a tradition at your Thanksgiving dinner, they should have a place in the day's festivities. These cranberry and nut-studded cookies will quiet the predinner hungries or top off a late evening snack. Fall Harvest Oatmeal Cookies will make a great dessert for even the most finicky kid on your guest list. No matter which you choose, these make-ahead treats are sure to please.

Aloha Oatmeal Cookies

If friends are embarking on a special trip, send them off in style with a Bon Voyage Party. Serve cookies that are appropriate to their destination. These spicy cookies loaded with pineapple, coconut and macadamia nuts are great whether their destination is Hawaii or some other island paradise. Since cookies are such great travelers, wrap the extras for snacking on the trip.

1¼ cups firmly packed light brown sugar
¾ cup Butter Flavor Crisco all-vegetable shortening or ¾ Butter Flavor Crisco Stick
1 egg
2 tablespoons orange juice
1 tablespoon grated orange peel
1 teaspoon vanilla
½ teaspoon orange or lemon extract
3 cups quick oats, uncooked
1 cup all-purpose flour
½ teaspoon baking soda
½ teaspoon salt
½ teaspoon ground ginger
1 can (8 ounces) crushed pineapple in natural juice, well-drained
1 cup flaked coconut
1 cup chopped macadamia nuts

1. Heat oven to 375°F. Grease baking sheets. Place sheets of foil on countertop for cooling cookies.

2. Place brown sugar, shortening, egg, orange juice, orange peel, vanilla and orange extract in large bowl. Beat at medium speed of electric mixer until well blended.

3. Combine oats, flour, baking soda, salt and ginger. Add to shortening mixture; beat at low speed just until blended. Stir in pineapple, coconut and macadamia nuts.

4. Drop dough by rounded measuring tablespoonfuls 2 inches apart onto prepared baking sheets.

5. Bake one baking sheet at a time at 375°F for 10 to 12 minutes or until cookies are lightly browned. *Do not overbake.* Cool 2 minutes. Remove cookies to foil to cool.
Makes about 2½ dozen cookies

Aloha Oatmeal Cookies

Oatmeal Praline Cheese Bars

Cookie Base

1¼ cups firmly packed light
  brown sugar
¾ cup Butter Flavor Crisco
  all-vegetable shortening
  or ¾ Butter Flavor
  Crisco Stick
1 egg
⅓ cup milk
1½ teaspoons vanilla
1½ cups quick oats, uncooked
1 cup all-purpose flour
1 cup finely chopped pecans
¼ cup toasted wheat germ
½ teaspoon baking soda
½ teaspoon salt
½ teaspoon cinnamon

Topping

1 package (8 ounces) cream
  cheese, softened
⅓ cup firmly packed light
  brown sugar
2 eggs
2 tablespoons all-purpose
  flour
½ teaspoon vanilla
¼ teaspoon salt
½ cup almond brickle chips
½ cup finely chopped pecans

1. Heat oven to 350°F. Grease 13 × 9-inch baking pan. Place cooling rack on countertop.

2. For cookie base, place brown sugar, shortening, egg, milk and vanilla in large bowl. Beat at medium speed of electric mixer until well blended.

3. Combine oats, flour, pecans, wheat germ, baking soda, salt and cinnamon. Add to shortening mixture; beat at low speed just until blended.

4. Spread dough onto bottom of prepared pan.

5. Bake at 350°F for 15 to 17 minutes or until surface is light golden brown and edges pull away from sides of pan. *Do not overbake.*

6. For topping, place cream cheese, brown sugar, eggs, flour, vanilla and salt in medium bowl. Beat at medium speed of electric mixer until smooth. Pour mixture over cookie base. Sprinkle with almond brickle chips and pecans.

7. Bake 15 to 17 minutes longer or until topping is set. *Do not overbake.* Cool completely on cooling rack. Cut into 2 × 1½-inch bars. Refrigerate.

Makes about 3 dozen bars

*Top to bottom: Cappuccino Cookies
(page 58), Oatmeal Praline
Cheese Bars*

Chocolate Cherry Oatmeal Fancies

Everyone loves cookie baking and spending time with loved ones around the holidays. Why not combine the two and invite a group for a cookie-baking session? Ask your guests to bring their favorite recipes. Spend the day baking and everyone goes home with a fantastic assortment of cookies.

½ cup sliced almonds
1¼ cups firmly packed light brown sugar
¾ cup Butter Flavor Crisco all-vegetable shortening or ¾ Butter Flavor Crisco Stick
1 egg
⅓ cup milk
1 teaspoon vanilla
½ teaspoon almond extract
3 cups quick oats, uncooked
1 cup all-purpose flour
½ teaspoon baking soda
½ teaspoon salt
6 ounces white baking chocolate, coarsely chopped
6 ounces semisweet chocolate, coarsely chopped
½ cup coarsely chopped red candied cherries or well-drained, chopped maraschino cherries

1. Heat oven to 350°F. Spread almonds on baking sheet. Bake at 350°F for 5 to 7 minutes or until almonds are golden brown. Cool completely; reserve.

2. *Increase oven temperature to 375°F.* Grease baking sheets. Place sheets of foil on countertop for cooling cookies.

3. Place brown sugar, shortening, egg, milk, vanilla and almond extract in large bowl. Beat at medium speed of electric mixer until well blended.

4. Combine oats, flour, baking soda and salt. Add to shortening mixture; beat at low speed just until blended. Stir in white chocolate, semisweet chocolate, cherries and reserved almonds.

5. Drop dough by rounded measuring tablespoonfuls 2 inches apart onto prepared baking sheets.

6. Bake one baking sheet at a time at 375°F for 10 to 12 minutes or until cookies are lightly browned. *Do not overbake.* Cool 2 minutes on baking sheet. Remove cookies to foil to cool completely.

Makes about 4 dozen cookies

Good 'n' Tasties

1¼ cups firmly packed light brown sugar
¾ cup Butter Flavor Crisco all-vegetable shortening or ¾ Butter Flavor Crisco Stick
1 egg
⅓ cup milk
1 tablespoon grated orange peel
1½ teaspoons vanilla
1½ cups quick oats, uncooked
1 cup whole-wheat flour

½ cup all-purpose flour
¼ cup toasted wheat germ
1½ teaspoons cinnamon
1 teaspoon baking soda
½ teaspoon salt
1 cup raisins
1 cup coarsely chopped walnuts or pecans
1 apple, peeled and coarsely chopped
½ cup grated carrots
½ cup flaked coconut

1. Heat oven to 375°F. Grease baking sheets. Place sheets of foil on countertop for cooling cookies.

2. Place brown sugar, shortening, egg, milk, orange peel and vanilla in large bowl. Beat at medium speed of electric mixer until well blended.

3. Combine oats, whole-wheat flour, all-purpose flour, wheat germ, cinnamon, baking soda and salt. Add to shortening mixture; beat at low speed just until blended. Stir in raisins, walnuts, apple, carrots and coconut.

4. Drop dough by rounded measuring tablespoonfuls 2 inches apart onto prepared baking sheets.

5. Bake one baking sheet at a time at 375°F for 10 to 12 minutes or until cookies are lightly browned. *Do not overbake.* Cool 2 minutes on baking sheet. Remove cookies to foil to cool completely.

Makes about 3½ dozen cookies

Peach Oatmeal Bars

Summer is naturally a time for friends and family to gather. Plan a picnic or barbecue for Memorial Day, Fourth of July or Labor Day. Just be sure the menu includes an assortment of easy-to-transport cookies—chewy Peach Oatmeal Bars, refreshing Tropical Lime Cookies or Cracked Chocolate Cookies loaded with bits of chocolate.

1¼ cups firmly packed light brown sugar
¾ cup Butter Flavor Crisco all-vegetable shortening or ¾ Butter Flavor Crisco Stick
1 egg
2 tablespoons milk
1 teaspoon vanilla
½ teaspoon almond extract
3 cups quick oats, uncooked
1 cup all-purpose flour
½ teaspoon baking soda
½ teaspoon salt
½ teaspoon ground ginger
1 can (16 ounces) sliced peaches, drained and finely chopped
1 cup peach preserves or jam, stirred

1. Heat oven to 350°F. Grease 15½ × 10½ × 1-inch jelly-roll pan.

2. Place brown sugar, shortening, egg, milk, vanilla and almond extract in large bowl. Beat at medium speed of electric mixer until well blended.

3. Combine oats, flour, baking soda, salt and ginger. Add to shortening mixture; beat at low speed just until blended. Stir in chopped peaches.

4. Spread ½ of dough onto bottom of prepared pan. Spread preserves over dough. Drop remaining dough by spoonfuls over preserves. Spread dough.

5. Bake at 350°F for 30 to 35 minutes or until golden brown. *Do not overbake.* Loosen from sides of pan with knife. Cool completely on cooling rack. Cut into 2 × 1½-inch bars.   *Makes about 4 dozen bars*

Clockwise from top left: Peach Oatmeal Bars, Cracked Chocolate Cookies (page 90), Tropical Lime Cookies (page 59)

Chewy Oatmeal Trail Mix Cookies

1¼ cups firmly packed light brown
    sugar
¾ cup Butter Flavor Crisco all-
    vegetable shortening or ¾ Butter
    Flavor Crisco Stick
1 egg
⅓ cup milk
1½ teaspoons vanilla
2½ cups quick oats, uncooked
1 cup all-purpose flour
½ teaspoon baking soda
½ teaspoon salt
¼ teaspoon cinnamon
1 cup (6 ounces) semisweet or milk
    chocolate chips
¾ cup raisins
¾ cup coarsely chopped nuts
½ cup sunflower seeds

1. Heat oven to 375°F. Grease baking sheets. Place sheets of foil on countertop.

2. Place brown sugar, shortening, egg, milk and vanilla in large bowl. Beat at medium speed of electric mixer until well blended.

3. Combine oats, flour, baking soda, salt and cinnamon. Add to shortening mixture; beat at low speed just until blended. Stir in chocolate chips, raisins, nuts and sunflower seeds.

4. Drop dough by rounded measuring tablespoonfuls 2 inches apart onto prepared baking sheets.

5. Bake one baking sheet at a time at 375°F for 10 to 12 minutes or until cookies are lightly browned. *Do not overbake.* Cool 2 minutes. Remove cookies to foil to cool completely.   *Makes about 3 dozen cookies*

These cookies will practically beg to be taken along on your next camping or hiking expedition or trip to the beach. They are chock-full of goodies that will satisfy your hunger.

Three cups of prepared trail mix (available in grocery or health food stores) can be substituted for the chocolate chips, raisins, nuts and sunflower seeds.

Chewy Oatmeal Trail Mix Cookies

ULTIMATE SUGAR COOKIES

In the past, sugar cookies were primarily seen as blank canvases begging to be decorated for the holidays. Although pretty, few of us liked the flavor or texture of the cookie. Now meet the Ultimate Sugar Cookie! It was developed by the Crisco Kitchens to be so moist, and above all so delectable, that it will become one of your favorites. And now it is less likely to crumble when iced than a crisper cookie made with butter or margarine. This makes it the ideal cookie for cutting into shapes and decorating.

Browse through this chapter and discover how versatile this recipe can be. With minor variations, you can have a great array of scrumptious cookies in a seemingly endless variety of shapes. You and your family can travel the world right in your kitchen—from the intriguing Scandinavian flavor of Orange-Cardamom Thins to Southwestern Bizcochitos, fragrant with anise. And don't miss the delightful Jammy Pinwheels and fantastic Frosted Easter Cut-outs.

So forget your old notions about sugar cookies and discover the whole new world of Ultimate Sugar Cookies—dazzling to the taste buds and exquisite to behold.

Ultimate Sugar Cookies (page 48)

Ultimate Sugar Cookies

1¼ cups granulated sugar
1 cup Butter Flavor Crisco
    all-vegetable shortening
    or 1 Butter Flavor
    Crisco Stick
2 eggs
¼ cup light corn syrup or
    regular pancake syrup
1 tablespoon vanilla

3 cups all-purpose flour
    (plus 4 tablespoons),
    divided
¾ teaspoon baking powder
½ teaspoon baking soda
½ teaspoon salt
    Granulated sugar or
    colored sugar crystals

1. Place sugar and shortening in large bowl. Beat at medium speed of electric mixer until well blended. Add eggs, syrup and vanilla; beat until well blended and fluffy.

2. Combine 3 cups flour, baking powder, baking soda and salt. Add gradually to shortening mixture, beating at low speed until well blended.

3. Divide dough into 4 equal pieces; shape each piece into disk. Wrap with plastic wrap. Refrigerate 1 hour or until firm.

4. Heat oven to 375°F. Place sheets of foil on countertop for cooling cookies.

5. Sprinkle about 1 tablespoon flour on large sheet of waxed paper. Place disk of dough on floured paper; flatten slightly with hands. Turn dough over; cover with another large sheet of waxed paper. Roll dough to ¼-inch thickness. Remove top sheet of waxed paper. Cut into desired shapes with floured cookie cutters. Place 2 inches apart on ungreased baking sheet. Repeat with remaining dough.

6. Sprinkle with granulated sugar.

7. Bake one baking sheet at a time at 375°F for 5 to 7 minutes or until edges of cookies are lightly browned. *Do not overbake.* Cool 2 minutes on baking sheet. Remove cookies to foil to cool completely.

Makes about 3½ dozen cookies

Orange-Cardamom Thins

1¼ cups granulated sugar
1 cup Butter Flavor Crisco
    all-vegetable shortening
    or 1 Butter Flavor Crisco Stick
1 egg
¼ cup light corn syrup or regular
    pancake syrup
1 teaspoon vanilla
1 tablespoon grated orange peel
½ teaspoon orange extract
3 cups all-purpose flour
1¼ teaspoons cardamom
¾ teaspoon baking powder
½ teaspoon baking soda
½ teaspoon salt
½ teaspoon cinnamon

1. Place sugar and shortening in large bowl. Beat at medium speed of electric mixer until well blended. Add egg, syrup, vanilla, orange peel and orange extract; beat until well blended and fluffy.

2. Combine flour, cardamom, baking powder, baking soda, salt and cinnamon. Add gradually to shortening mixture, beating at low speed until well blended.

3. Divide dough in half. Roll each half into 12-inch-long log. Wrap with plastic wrap. Refrigerate for 4 hours or until firm.

4. Heat oven to 375°F. Grease baking sheets. Place sheets of foil on counter for cooling cookies.

5. Cut rolls into ¼-inch-thick slices. Place 1 inch apart on prepared baking sheets.

6. Bake one baking sheet at a time at 375°F for 7 to 9 minutes or until bottoms of cookies are lightly browned. *Do not overbake.* Cool 2 minutes on baking sheet. Remove cookies to foil to cool completely.
    Makes about 5 dozen cookies

Cardamom, a member of the ginger family, has a pungent aroma and a spicy-sweet flavor. It is used most often in Scandinavian and East Indian cooking.

Toffee Spattered Sugar Stars

1¼ cups granulated sugar
1 cup Butter Flavor Crisco
    all-vegetable shortening
    or 1 Butter Flavor
    Crisco Stick
2 eggs
¼ cup light corn syrup or
    regular pancake syrup
1 tablespoon vanilla

3 cups all-purpose flour
    (plus 4 tablespoons),
    divided
¾ teaspoon baking powder
½ teaspoon baking soda
½ teaspoon salt
1 package (6 ounces) milk
    chocolate English toffee
    chips, divided

1. Place sugar and shortening in large bowl. Beat at medium speed of electric mixer until well blended. Add eggs, syrup and vanilla; beat until well blended and fluffy.

2. Combine 3 cups flour, baking powder, baking soda and salt. Add gradually to shortening mixture, beating at low speed until well blended.

3. Divide dough into 4 equal pieces; shape each into disk. Wrap with plastic wrap. Refrigerate 1 hour or until firm.

4. Heat oven to 375°F. Place sheets of foil on countertop for cooling cookies.

5. Sprinkle about 1 tablespoon flour on large sheet of waxed paper. Place disk of dough on floured paper; flatten slightly with hands. Turn dough over; cover with another large sheet of waxed paper. Roll dough to ¼-inch thickness. Remove top sheet of waxed paper. Sprinkle about ¼ of toffee chips over dough. Roll lightly into dough. Cut out with floured star or round cookie cutter. Place 2 inches apart on ungreased baking sheet. Repeat with remaining dough and toffee chips.

6. Bake one baking sheet at a time at 375°F for 5 to 7 minutes or until cookies are lightly browned around edges. *Do not overbake.* Cool 2 minutes on baking sheet. Remove cookies to foil to cool completely.

Makes about 3½ dozen cookies

Top to bottom: Pecan Cookies (page 58), *Toffee Spattered Sugar Stars*

Jammy Pinwheels

1¼ cups granulated sugar
1 cup Butter Flavor Crisco
   all-vegetable shortening
   or 1 Butter Flavor
   Crisco Stick
2 eggs
¼ cup light corn syrup or
   regular pancake syrup
1 tablespoon vanilla

3 cups all-purpose flour
   (plus 2 tablespoons),
   divided
¾ teaspoon baking powder
½ teaspoon baking soda
½ teaspoon salt
1 cup apricot, strawberry or
   seedless raspberry jam

1. Place sugar and shortening in large bowl. Beat at medium speed of electric mixer until well blended. Add eggs, syrup and vanilla; beat until well blended and fluffy.

2. Combine 3 cups flour, baking powder, baking soda and salt. Add gradually to shortening mixture, beating at low speed until well blended.

3. Divide dough in half. Pat each half into thick rectangle. Sprinkle about 1 tablespoon flour on large sheet of waxed paper. Place rectangle of dough on floured paper. Turn dough over; cover with another large sheet of waxed paper. Roll dough into an 8 × 12-inch rectangle about ⅛ inch thick. Trim edges. Slide dough and waxed paper onto ungreased baking sheets. Refrigerate 20 minutes or until firm. Repeat with remaining dough.

4. Heat oven to 375°F. Grease baking sheets. Place sheets of foil on counter for cooling cookies.

5. Place chilled dough rectangle on work surface. Remove top sheet of waxed paper. Cut dough into 2-inch squares. Place squares 2 inches apart on prepared baking sheets. Make a 1-inch diagonal cut from each corner of square almost to center. Place 1 teaspoon jam in center. Lift every other corner and bring together in center of cookie. Repeat with remaining dough.

6. Bake at 375°F for 7 to 10 minutes or until edges of cookies are golden brown. *Do not overbake.* Cool 2 minutes on baking sheet. Remove cookies to foil to cool completely.

Makes about 4 dozen cookies

Clockwise from top left: Jammy Pinwheels, Chocolate Cherry Oatmeal Fancies (page 40), *Southwestern Bizcochitos* (page 54)

Southwestern Bizcochitos

Cookies

1¼ cups granulated sugar
1 cup Butter Flavor Crisco
    all-vegetable shortening
    or 1 Butter Flavor
    Crisco Stick
2 eggs
¼ cup light corn syrup or
    regular pancake syrup
1 tablespoon vanilla
1 tablespoon grated orange
    peel
2 teaspoons anise seed

3 cups all-purpose flour
    (plus 4 tablespoons),
    divided
¾ teaspoon baking powder
½ teaspoon baking soda
½ teaspoon salt

Topping

⅓ cup granulated sugar
1 tablespoon cinnamon
    Milk

1. For cookies, place sugar and shortening in large bowl. Beat at medium speed of electric mixer until well blended. Add eggs, syrup, vanilla, orange peel and anise seed; beat until well blended and fluffy.

2. Combine 3 cups flour, baking powder, baking soda and salt. Add gradually to shortening mixture, beating at low speed until well blended. Wrap dough in plastic wrap. Refrigerate 1 hour or overnight.

3. Divide dough into 4 equal pieces; shape each into a disk. Wrap with plastic wrap. Refrigerate 1 hour or until firm.

4. Heat oven to 375°F. Place sheets of foil on countertop for cooling cookies.

5. Sprinkle about 1 tablespoon of flour on large sheet of waxed paper. Place disk of dough on floured paper; flatten slightly with hands. Turn dough over; cover with another large sheet of waxed paper. Roll dough to ¼-inch thickness. Remove top sheet of waxed paper. Cut out with floured cookie cutter. Place 2 inches apart on ungreased baking sheet. Repeat with remaining dough.

6. For topping, combine sugar and cinnamon. Brush cookies with milk. Sprinkle cookies with sugar mixture.

7. Bake one baking sheet at a time at 375°F for 7 to 9 minutes or until cookies are lightly set. *Do not overbake.* Cool 2 minutes on baking sheet. Remove cookies to foil to cool completely.

Makes about 4½ dozen cookies

Spritz Cookies

1¼ cups granulated sugar
1 cup Butter Flavor Crisco
   all-vegetable shortening
   or 1 Butter Flavor
   Crisco Stick
2 eggs
¼ cup light corn syrup or
   regular pancake syrup
1 tablespoon vanilla

3 cups all-purpose flour
¾ teaspoon baking powder
½ teaspoon baking soda
½ teaspoon salt
   Colored sugar crystals
   (optional)
   Nonpareils (optional)
   Chocolate jimmies
   (optional)

1. Heat oven to 375°F. Place sheets of foil on countertop for cooling cookies.

2. Place sugar and shortening in large bowl. Beat at medium speed of electric mixer until well blended. Add eggs, syrup and vanilla; beat until well blended and fluffy.

3. Combine flour, baking powder, baking soda and salt. Add gradually to shortening mixture; beat at low speed until well blended.

4. Fill cookie press with dough, following manufacturer's directions. Press dough about 1½ inches apart on ungreased baking sheet. Sprinkle with colored sugar, nonpareils or chocolate jimmies, if desired.

5. Bake one sheet at a time at 375°F for 7 to 9 minutes or until bottoms of cookies are golden. *Do not overbake.* Cool 2 minutes on baking sheet. Remove cookies to foil to cool completely.
Makes about 7½ dozen cookies

Frosted Easter Cut-outs

Cookies

1¼ cups granulated sugar
1 cup Butter Flavor Crisco all-vegetable shortening or 1 Butter Flavor Crisco Stick
2 eggs
¼ cup light corn syrup or regular pancake syrup
1 tablespoon vanilla
3 cups all-purpose flour (plus 4 tablespoons), divided

¾ teaspoon baking powder
½ teaspoon baking soda
½ teaspoon salt

Icing

1 cup confectioners sugar
2 tablespoons milk
Food color (optional)
Decorating icing

1. Place sugar and shortening in large bowl. Beat at medium speed of electric mixer until well blended. Add eggs, syrup and vanilla; beat until well blended and fluffy.

2. Combine 3 cups flour, baking powder, baking soda and salt. Add gradually to shortening mixture, beating at low speed until well blended.

3. Divide dough into 4 equal pieces; shape each into disk. Wrap with plastic wrap. Refrigerate 1 hour or until firm.

4. Heat oven to 375°F. Place sheets of foil on countertop for cooling cookies.

5. Sprinkle about 1 tablespoon flour on large sheet of waxed paper. Place disk of dough on floured paper; flatten slightly with hands. Turn dough over; cover with another large sheet of waxed paper. Roll dough to ¼-inch thickness. Remove top sheet of waxed paper. Cut into desired shapes with floured cookie cutter. Place 2 inches apart on ungreased baking sheet. Repeat with remaining dough.

6. Bake one baking sheet at a time at 375°F for 5 to 7 minutes or until edges of cookies are lightly browned. *Do not overbake.* Cool 2 minutes on baking sheet. Remove cookies to foil to cool completely.

7. For icing, combine confectioners sugar and milk; stir until smooth. Add food color, if desired. Stir until blended. Spread icing on cookies; place on foil until icing is set. Decorate as desired with decorating icing.

Makes about 3½ dozen cookies

Pecan Cookies

1¼ cups confectioners sugar
1 cup Butter Flavor Crisco all-vegetable shortening or 1 Butter Flavor Crisco Stick
2 eggs
¼ cup light corn syrup or regular pancake syrup

1 tablespoon vanilla
2 cups all-purpose flour
1½ cups finely chopped pecans
¾ teaspoon baking powder
½ teaspoon baking soda
½ teaspoon salt
Confectioners sugar

1. Heat oven to 375°F. Place sheets of foil on countertop for cooling cookies.

2. Place 1¼ cups confectioners sugar and shortening in large bowl. Beat at medium speed of electric mixer until well blended. Add eggs, syrup and vanilla; beat until well blended and fluffy.

3. Combine flour, pecans, baking powder, baking soda and salt. Add to shortening mixture; beat at low speed until well blended.

4. Shape dough into 1-inch balls. Place 2 inches apart on ungreased baking sheet.

5. Bake at 375°F for 7 to 9 minutes or until bottoms of cookies are light golden brown. *Do not overbake.* Cool 2 minutes on baking sheet. Roll in confectioners sugar while warm. Remove cookies to foil to cool completely. Reroll in confectioners sugar just before serving.

Makes about 4 dozen cookies

Cappuccino Cookies

1¼ cups firmly packed light brown sugar
1 cup Butter Flavor Crisco all-vegetable shortening or 1 Butter Flavor Crisco Stick
2 eggs
¼ cup light corn syrup or regular pancake syrup
1 teaspoon vanilla

1 teaspoon rum extract
2 tablespoons instant espresso or coffee powder
3 cups all-purpose flour
¾ teaspoon baking powder
½ teaspoon baking soda
½ teaspoon salt
½ teaspoon nutmeg
Chocolate jimmies

1. Place brown sugar and shortening in large bowl. Beat at medium speed of electric mixer until well blended. Add eggs, corn syrup, vanilla, rum extract and coffee; beat until well blended and fluffy.

2. Combine flour, baking powder, baking soda, salt and nutmeg. Add gradually to shortening mixture, beating at low speed until blended. Divide dough in half. Roll each half into two logs approximately 2 inches in diameter. Wrap in waxed paper. Refrigerate several hours.

3. Heat oven to 375°F. Place sheets of foil on countertop for cooling cookies.

4. Cut cookies into ¼-inch-thick slices. Place 2 inches apart on ungreased baking sheet. Sprinkle center of each cookie with jimmies.

5. Bake one baking sheet at a time at 375°F for 7 to 9 minutes or until golden brown. *Do not overbake.* Cool 2 minutes. Remove cookies to foil to cool completely. *Makes about 4½ dozen cookies*

Tropical Lime Cookies

1¼ cups confectioners sugar
1 cup Butter Flavor Crisco all-vegetable shortening or 1 Butter Flavor Crisco Stick
1 egg
¼ cup light corn syrup or regular pancake syrup
2 tablespoons lime juice
2 tablespoons grated lime peel (about 2 limes)
2½ cups all-purpose flour
¾ teaspoon baking powder
½ teaspoon baking soda
½ teaspoon salt
1 cup flaked coconut
Confectioners sugar

1. Heat oven to 325°F. Place sheets of foil on countertop for cooling cookies.

2. Place confectioners sugar and shortening in large bowl. Beat at medium speed of electric mixer until well blended. Add egg, syrup, lime juice and lime peel; beat until well blended and fluffy.

3. Combine flour, baking powder, baking soda and salt. Add gradually to shortening mixture, beating at low speed until well blended. Stir in coconut.

4. Shape dough into 1-inch balls. Place 2 inches apart on ungreased baking sheet.

5. Bake one baking sheet at a time at 325°F for 15 to 18 minutes or until bottoms of cookies are light golden brown. *Do not overbake.* Cool 2 minutes on baking sheet. Remove cookies to foil. Dust warm cookies with confectioners sugar. Cool completely. Garnish as desired. *Makes about 5 dozen cookies*

Maple Pecan Sandwich Cookies

Cookies

1¼ cups firmly packed light brown sugar
1 cup Butter Flavor Crisco all-vegetable shortening or 1 Butter Flavor Crisco Stick
2 eggs
¼ cup maple syrup or maple flavored pancake syrup
1 teaspoon maple extract
½ teaspoon vanilla
2½ cups all-purpose flour (plus 4 tablespoons), divided
1½ cups finely ground pecans

¾ teaspoon baking powder
½ teaspoon baking soda
½ teaspoon salt
20 to 30 pecan halves (optional)

Filling

1¼ cups confectioners sugar
3 tablespoons Butter Flavor Crisco all-vegetable shortening
1 teaspoon maple extract
Dash salt
2½ teaspoons milk

1. For cookies, place brown sugar and shortening in large bowl. Beat at medium speed of electric mixer until well blended. Add eggs, syrup, maple extract and vanilla; beat until well blended and fluffy.

2. Combine 2½ cups flour, ground pecans, baking powder, baking soda and salt. Add gradually to shortening mixture, beating at low speed until well blended. Divide dough into 4 equal pieces; shape each into disk. Wrap with plastic wrap. Refrigerate 1 hour or until firm.

3. Heat oven to 375°F. Place sheets of foil on countertop for cooling cookies.

4. Sprinkle about 1 tablespoon flour on large sheet of waxed paper. Place disk of dough on floured paper; flatten slightly with hands. Turn dough over; cover with another large sheet of waxed paper. Roll dough to ¼-inch thickness. Cut out with floured 3-inch scalloped round cookie cutter. Place 2 inches apart on ungreased baking sheet. Roll out remaining dough. Place pecans in center of half of cookies, if desired.

5. Bake one baking sheet at a time at 375°F for 5 to 7 minutes or until lightly browned around edges. *Do not overbake.* Cool 2 minutes on baking sheet. Remove cookies to foil to cool completely.

6. For filling, place confectioners sugar, shortening, maple extract and salt in medium bowl. Beat at low speed until smooth. Add milk; beat until mixture is smooth. Spread filling on flat side of 1 plain cookie. Cover with flat side of second cookie with pecan. Repeat with remaining cookies and filling. Garnish as desired.

Makes about 2 dozen sandwich cookies

Raspberry Linzer Rounds

1¼ cups granulated sugar
1 cup Butter Flavor Crisco
   all-vegetable shortening
   or 1 Butter Flavor
   Crisco Stick
2 eggs
¼ cup light corn syrup or
   regular pancake syrup
1 teaspoon vanilla
1 teaspoon almond extract
3 cups all-purpose flour
   (plus 4 tablespoons),
   divided

1 cup ground almonds
   (about 4 to 5 ounces)
¾ teaspoon baking powder
½ teaspoon baking soda
½ teaspoon salt
½ cup seedless raspberry
   preserves, stirred
Confectioners sugar
   (optional)

1. Place granulated sugar and shortening in large bowl. Beat at medium speed of electric mixer until well blended. Add eggs, syrup, vanilla and almond extract; beat until well blended and fluffy.

2. Combine 3 cups flour, ground almonds, baking powder, baking soda and salt. Add gradually to shortening mixture, beating at low speed until well blended.

3. Divide dough into 4 pieces; shape each piece into disk. Wrap with plastic wrap. Refrigerate several hours or until firm.

4. Heat oven to 375°F. Place sheets of foil on countertop for cooling cookies.

5. Sprinkle about 1 tablespoon flour on large sheet of waxed paper. Place disk of dough on floured paper; flatten slightly with hands. Turn dough over and cover with another large sheet of waxed paper. Roll dough to ¼-inch thickness. Remove top sheet of waxed paper. Cut out with 2- or 2½-inch floured scalloped round cookie cutter. Place 2 inches apart on ungreased baking sheet. Repeat with remaining dough. Cut out centers of half the cookies with ½- or ¾-inch round cutter.

6. Bake one baking sheet at a time at 375°F for 5 to 7 minutes or until edges of cookies are lightly browned.* *Do not overbake.* Cool 2 minutes on baking sheet. Remove cookies to foil to cool completely.

7. Spread a small amount of raspberry jam on bottom of solid cookies; cover with cut-out cookies, bottom sides down, to form sandwiches. Sift confectioners sugar, if desired, over tops of cookies.

Makes about 2 dozen cookies

*Bake larger cookies 1 to 2 minutes longer.

St. Pat's Pinwheels

1¼ cups granulated sugar
1 cup Butter Flavor Crisco
all-vegetable shortening
or 1 Butter Flavor
Crisco Stick
2 eggs
¼ cup light corn syrup or
regular pancake syrup
1 tablespoon vanilla

3 cups all-purpose flour
(plus 2 tablespoons),
divided
¾ teaspoon baking powder
½ teaspoon baking soda
½ teaspoon salt
½ teaspoon peppermint
extract
Green food color

1. Place sugar and shortening in large bowl. Beat at medium speed of electric mixer until well blended. Add eggs, syrup and vanilla; beat until well blended and fluffy.

2. Combine 3 cups flour, baking powder, baking soda and salt. Add gradually to shortening mixture, beating at low speed until well blended.

3. Place half of dough in medium bowl. Stir in peppermint extract and food color, a few drops at a time, until of desired shade of green. Shape each dough into disk. Wrap with plastic wrap. Refrigerate several hours or until firm.

4. Sprinkle about 1 tablespoon flour on large sheet of waxed paper. Place peppermint dough on floured paper; flatten slightly with hands. Turn dough over; cover with another large sheet of waxed paper. Roll dough into 14 × 9-inch rectangle. Set aside. Repeat with plain dough.

5. Remove top sheet of waxed paper from both doughs. Invert plain dough onto peppermint dough, aligning edges carefully. Roll layers together lightly. Remove waxed paper from plain dough. Trim dough to form rectangle. Roll dough tightly in jelly-roll fashion starting with long side and using bottom sheet of waxed paper as guide, removing waxed paper during rolling. Wrap roll in waxed paper; freeze at least 30 minutes or until very firm.

6. Heat oven to 375°F. Place sheets of foil on countertop for cooling cookies.

7. Remove roll from freezer; remove wrapping. Cut roll into ⅜-inch-thick slices. Place slices 2 inches apart on ungreased baking sheet.

8. Bake one baking sheet at a time at 375°F for 7 to 9 minutes or until edges of cookies are very lightly browned. *Do not overbake.* Cool 2 minutes on baking sheet. Remove cookies to foil to cool completely.
Makes about 3 dozen cookies

St. Pat's Pinwheels

Lollipop Cookies

Cookies

1¼ cups granulated sugar
1 cup Butter Flavor Crisco
    all-vegetable shortening
    or 1 Butter Flavor
    Crisco Stick
2 eggs
¼ cup light corn syrup or
    regular pancake syrup
1 tablespoon vanilla
3 cups all-purpose flour
¾ teaspoon baking powder
½ teaspoon baking soda
½ teaspoon salt
36 flat ice cream sticks

Decorations

Any of the following:
    miniature baking chips,
    raisins, red hots,
    nonpareils, colored
    sugar or nuts

1. Place sugar and shortening in large bowl. Beat at medium speed of electric mixer until well blended. Add eggs, syrup and vanilla; beat until well blended and fluffy.

2. Combine flour, baking powder, baking soda and salt. Add gradually to shortening mixture, beating at low speed until well blended. Cover; refrigerate for several hours or until firm.

3. Heat oven to 375°F. Place sheets of foil on countertop for cooling cookies.

4. Shape dough into 1½-inch balls. Push ice cream stick into center of dough. Place dough 3 inches apart on ungreased baking sheet with stick parallel to baking sheet. Flatten dough to ½-inch thickness with bottom of greased and floured glass. Decorate as desired; press decorations gently into dough.

5. Bake at 375°F for 8 to 10 minutes. *Do not overbake.* Cool on baking sheet 2 minutes. Remove cookies to foil to cool completely.

Makes about 3 dozen cookies

Lemon-Poppy Seed Cookies

1¼ cups granulated sugar
1 cup Butter Flavor Crisco all-vegetable shortening or 1 Butter Flavor Crisco Stick
2 eggs
¼ cup light corn syrup or regular pancake syrup
2 tablespoons poppy seeds
1 tablespoon grated lemon peel

1½ teaspoons pure lemon extract
1 teaspoon vanilla
3 cups all-purpose flour (plus 4 tablespoons), divided
1 teaspoon ground ginger
¾ teaspoon baking powder
½ teaspoon baking soda
½ teaspoon salt

1. Place sugar and shortening in large bowl. Beat at medium speed of electric mixer until well blended. Add eggs, syrup, poppy seeds, lemon peel, lemon extract and vanilla; beat until well blended and fluffy.

2. Combine 3 cups flour, ginger, baking powder, baking soda and salt. Add gradually to shortening mixture, beating at low speed until well blended.

3. Divide dough into 4 equal pieces; shape each piece into disk. Wrap with plastic wrap. Refrigerate 1 hour or until firm.

4. Heat oven to 375°F. Place sheets of foil on countertop for cooling cookies.

5. Sprinkle about 1 tablespoon flour on large sheet of waxed paper. Place disk of dough on floured paper; flatten slightly with hands. Turn dough over; cover with another large sheet of waxed paper. Roll dough to ⅛-inch thickness. Remove top sheet of waxed paper. Cut out with floured scalloped round or heart cookie cutters. Place 2 inches apart on ungreased baking sheet. Repeat with remaining dough.

6. Bake one baking sheet at a time at 375°F for 5 to 6 minutes or until edges of cookies just begin to brown. *Do not overbake.* Cool 2 minutes on baking sheet. Remove cookies to foil to cool completely.

Makes about 6½ dozen cookies

IRRESISTIBLE PEANUT BUTTER COOKIES

Peanut butter cookies are instantly recognized by their familiar crosshatch pattern. But beneath those lines, Crisco's Irresistible Peanut Butter Cookies are brimming with peanut butter flavor. They deliver the maximum in peanut taste as well as the soft moist texture that you prefer.

While the basic Irresistible Peanut Butter Cookie is a favorite with everyone, the Crisco Kitchens have developed a number of quick variations with peanut butter as the star. Try Crunchy & Chippy Peanut Butter Cookies and savor the full-bodied peanut flavor. Or pair peanut butter with its traditional partners—chocolate in the dazzling but easy-to-make Inside-Out Peanut Butter Cookie Cups, jelly in kid-pleasing Peanut Butter Thumbprints and bananas in the memorable Bananaramas. In this chapter, peanut butter-flavored cookies are not confined to drop cookies. Use the basic dough to make unbeatable no-fuss Peanut Butter & Jelly Streusel Bars.

Discover the versatility of the basic Irresistible Peanut Butter Cookie recipe. Just turn the page and treat the kid in everyone to dynamic peanut butter creations.

Irresistible Peanut Butter Cookies
(page 68)

Irresistible Peanut Butter Cookies

1¼ cups firmly packed light
   brown sugar
¾ cup creamy peanut butter
½ cup Crisco all-vegetable
   shortening or ½ Crisco
   Stick

3 tablespoons milk
1 tablespoon vanilla
1 egg
1¾ cups all-purpose flour
¾ teaspoon baking soda
¾ teaspoon salt

1. Heat oven to 375°F. Place sheets of foil on countertop for cooling cookies.

2. Place brown sugar, peanut butter, shortening, milk and vanilla in large bowl. Beat at medium speed of electric mixer until well blended. Add egg; beat just until blended.

3. Combine flour, baking soda and salt. Add to shortening mixture; beat at low speed just until blended.

4. Drop dough by rounded measuring tablespoonfuls 2 inches apart onto ungreased baking sheet. Flatten dough slightly in crisscross pattern with tines of fork.

5. Bake one baking sheet at a time at 375°F for 7 to 8 minutes or until cookies are set and just beginning to brown. *Do not overbake*. Cool 2 minutes on baking sheet. Remove cookies to foil to cool completely.

Makes about 3 dozen cookies

Inside-Out Peanut Butter Cookie Cups

Cookies
1¼ cups firmly packed light brown sugar
¾ cup creamy peanut butter
½ cup Crisco all-vegetable shortening or ½ Crisco Stick
3 tablespoons milk
1 tablespoon vanilla
1 egg
1¾ cups all-purpose flour
¾ teaspoon baking soda
¾ teaspoon salt

Filling
1 cup (6 ounces) semi-sweet chocolate chips
1 teaspoon Butter Flavor Crisco all-vegetable shortening*
¼ cup finely chopped peanuts

*Crisco all-vegetable shortening can be substituted for Butter Flavor Crisco.

1. For cookies, place brown sugar, peanut butter, shortening, milk and vanilla in large bowl. Beat at medium speed of electric mixer until well blended. Add egg; beat just until blended.

2. Combine flour, baking soda and salt. Add to shortening mixture; beat at low speed just until blended. Refrigerate about 1 hour or until firm.

3. Heat oven to 375°F. Grease mini-muffin pans. Place sheets of foil on countertop for cooling cookies.

4. Shape dough into 1-inch balls. Place each ball in prepared mini-muffin cup (1¾ inches in diameter). Press dough onto bottom and sides of cup to within ½ inch of top.

5. Bake at 375°F for 7 to 8 minutes or until cookies are set and just beginning to brown. *Do not overbake.* Cool 10 minutes on cooling racks. Remove cookie cups carefully to foil to cool completely.

6. For filling, place chocolate chips and shortening in medium microwave-safe bowl. Microwave at 50% (MEDIUM) for 1 to 2 minutes or until chips are shiny and soft. Stir until smooth. Spoon about ½ teaspoon chocolate mixture into center of each cookie. Sprinkle with chopped peanuts. Cool completely.   *Makes about 3½ dozen cookie cups*

Bananaramas

1¼ cups firmly packed light
   brown sugar
¾ cup creamy peanut butter
½ cup Crisco all-vegetable
   shortening or ½ Crisco
   Stick
1 cup mashed banana
3 tablespoons milk
1½ teaspoons vanilla
½ teaspoon almond extract

1 egg
2 cups all-purpose flour
¾ teaspoon baking soda
¾ teaspoon salt
1½ cups milk chocolate
   chunks or semisweet
   chocolate chunks*
1 cup peanuts or coarsely
   chopped pecans
   (optional)

* A combination of milk chocolate and semisweet chocolate chunks can be used.

1. Heat oven to 350°F. Place sheets of foil on countertop for cooling cookies.

2. Place brown sugar, peanut butter, shortening, banana, milk, vanilla and almond extract in large bowl. Beat at medium speed of electric mixer until well blended. Add egg; beat just until blended.

3. Combine flour, baking soda and salt. Add to shortening mixture; beat at low speed just until blended. Stir in chocolate chunks and nuts, if desired.

4. Drop dough by rounded measuring tablespoonfuls 2 inches apart onto ungreased baking sheets.

5. Bake one baking sheet at a time at 350°F for 11 to 13 minutes or until cookies are light brown around edges. *Do not overbake.* Cool 2 minutes on baking sheet. Remove cookies to foil to cool completely.
Makes about 4 dozen cookies

*Top to bottom: Bananaramas,
Inside-Out Peanut Butter
Cookie Cups* (page 69)

Peanut Butter & Jelly Streusel Bars

1¼ cups firmly packed light brown
    sugar
¾ cup creamy peanut butter
½ cup Crisco all-vegetable shortening
    or ½ Crisco Stick
3 tablespoons milk
1 tablespoon vanilla
1 egg
1¾ cups all-purpose flour
¾ teaspoon baking soda
¾ teaspoon salt
1 cup strawberry jam, stirred
½ cup quick oats, uncooked

1. Heat oven to 350°F. Grease 13 × 9-inch baking pan. Place cooling rack on countertop.

2. Place brown sugar, peanut butter, shortening, milk and vanilla in large bowl. Beat at medium speed of electric mixer until well blended. Add egg; beat just until blended.

3. Combine flour, baking soda and salt. Add to shortening mixture; beat at low speed just until blended.

4. Press ⅔ of dough onto bottom of prepared baking pan. Spread jam over dough to within ¼ inch of edges.

5. Add oats to remaining dough. Drop dough by spoonfuls onto jam.

6. Bake at 350°F for 20 to 25 minutes or until edges and streusel topping are lightly browned. *Do not overbake.* Cool completely on cooling rack. Cut into 2 × 1½-inch bars.
Makes about 3 dozen bars

Clockwise from top left: Peanut Butter & Jelly Streusel Bars, Irresistible Peanut Butter Jack O' Lanterns (page 75), Peanut Butter Sombreros (page 74)

Plan a fun-filled Halloween party—it's easy to do and popular with any age group. For entertainment, choose from a seemingly endless list of games—from silly to goulish. Cookies are a perfect fit for your menu because they are quick to prepare and easy to serve. While everyone will love these Peanut Butter & Jelly Streusel Bars, most any cookies will be a hit.

Peanut Butter Sombreros

For even browning, place only one baking sheet at a time in the oven. If the oven does not heat evenly, turn the baking sheet halfway through baking time. Baking sheets can be reused for a second batch of cookies. Just be sure baking sheets have cooled to room temperature before using; otherwise, cookies will spread too much.

1¼ cups firmly packed light brown sugar
¾ cup creamy peanut butter
½ cup Crisco all-vegetable shortening or ½ Crisco Stick
3 tablespoons milk
1 tablespoon vanilla
1 egg
1¾ cups all-purpose flour
¾ teaspoon baking soda
¾ teaspoon salt
Granulated sugar
40 to 50 chocolate kisses, unwrapped

1. Heat oven to 375°F. Place sheets of foil on countertop for cooling cookies.

2. Place brown sugar, peanut butter, shortening, milk and vanilla in large bowl. Beat at medium speed of electric mixer until well blended. Add egg; beat just until blended.

3. Combine flour, baking soda and salt. Add to shortening mixture; beat at low speed just until blended.

4. Shape dough into 1-inch balls. Roll in granulated sugar. Place 2 inches apart on ungreased baking sheets.

5. Bake one baking sheet at a time at 375°F for 6 minutes. Press chocolate kiss into center of each cookie. Bake 3 minutes longer. *Do not overbake.* Cool 2 minutes on baking sheet. Remove cookies to foil to cool completely.   *Makes about 4 dozen cookies*

Irresistible Peanut Butter Jack O' Lanterns

Cookies

1¼ cups firmly packed light brown sugar
¾ cup creamy peanut butter
½ cup Crisco all-vegetable shortening or ½ Crisco Stick
3 tablespoons milk
1 tablespoon vanilla
1 egg
1¾ cups all-purpose flour
¾ teaspoon baking soda
¾ teaspoon salt

Icing

1 cup (6 ounces) semisweet chocolate chips
2 teaspoons Butter Flavor Crisco all-vegetable shortening*

*Crisco all-vegetable shortening can be substituted for Butter Flavor Crisco.

1. Heat oven to 375°F. Place sheets of foil on countertop for cooling cookies.

2. For cookies, place brown sugar, peanut butter, shortening, milk and vanilla in large bowl. Beat at medium speed of electric mixer until well blended. Add egg; beat just until blended.

3. Combine flour, baking soda and salt. Add to shortening mixture; beat at low speed just until blended.

4. Pinch off pieces of dough the size of walnuts. Shape into balls. Place 3 inches apart on ungreased baking sheet. Flatten each ball with bottom of glass to approximately ⅜-inch thickness. Form into pumpkin shape, making indentation on top of round. Pinch off very small piece of dough and roll to form small stem. Attach to top of cookie. Score dough with vertical lines with small, sharp knife to resemble pumpkin.

5. Bake one baking sheet at a time at 375°F for 7 to 8 minutes or until cookies are set and just beginning to brown. *Do not overbake.* Cool on baking sheet 2 minutes. Remove cookies to foil to cool completely.

6. For icing, place chocolate chips and shortening in heavy resealable sandwich bag; seal bag. Microwave at 50% (MEDIUM) for 1 minute. Knead bag. If necessary, microwave at 50% for another 30 seconds at a time until mixture is smooth when bag is kneaded. Cut small tip off corner of bag. Pipe lines and faces on cookies to resemble jack o' lanterns.

Makes about 3 dozen cookies

Crunchy & Chippy Peanut Butter Cookies

1¼ cups firmly packed light brown sugar
¾ cup crunchy peanut butter
½ cup Crisco all-vegetable shortening or ½ Crisco Stick
3 tablespoons milk
1 tablespoon vanilla

1 egg
1¾ cups all-purpose flour
¾ teaspoon baking soda
¾ teaspoon salt
1 cup (6 ounces) miniature semisweet chocolate chips
1 cup chopped peanuts*

*Salted, unsalted or dry roasted peanuts can be used.

1. Heat oven to 375°F. Place sheets of foil on countertop for cooling cookies.

2. Place brown sugar, peanut butter, shortening, milk and vanilla in large bowl. Beat at medium speed of electric mixer until well blended. Add egg; beat just until blended.

3. Combine flour, baking soda and salt. Add to shortening mixture; beat at low speed just until blended. Stir in miniature chocolate chips and peanuts.

4. Drop dough by rounded measuring tablespoonfuls 2 inches apart onto ungreased baking sheets. Flatten slightly with fingers.

5. Bake one baking sheet at a time at 375°F for 7 to 8 minutes or until cookies are set and just beginning to brown. *Do not overbake.* Cool 2 minutes on baking sheet. Remove cookies to foil to cool completely.

Makes about 3 dozen cookies

Top to bottom: Crunchy & Chippy Peanut Butter Cookies, Almond Mocha Cookie Bars (page 85)

CHEWY BROWNIE COOKIES

For a true chocolate lover, nothing compares with the rich chocolaty flavor of a brownie. And now that flavor has been captured in the Chewy Brownie Cookie, a luscious drop cookie with a double dose of chocolate. This cookie, developed by the Crisco Kitchens to be moist and chewy, is sure to please any chocoholic on your guest list.

Some of the variations in this chapter are drawn from time-honored, crowd-pleasing chocolate flavor combinations. Chocolate-Mint Brownie Cookies team two old favorites. Friends will love the richness of Caramel Nut Chocolate Cookies and German Chocolate Brownie Cookies. Chocolate is a natural with coffee and almonds in Almond Mocha Cookie Bars. Or, press this basic chewy brownie dough into a baking pan and top with a cream cheese layer for heavenly Chocolate Cheesecake Bars.

Chocolate cookies are always welcome at any holiday celebration or special occasion. Explore this dark and fudgy collection of brownie cookie variations today. You will find inspiration at every turn.

Chewy Brownie Cookies (page 82)

Chewy Brownie Cookies

1½ cups firmly packed light brown sugar
⅔ cup Crisco all-vegetable shortening or ⅔ Crisco Stick
1 tablespoon water
1 teaspoon vanilla
2 eggs

1½ cups all-purpose flour
⅓ cup unsweetened cocoa powder
½ teaspoon salt
¼ teaspoon baking soda
2 cups (12 ounces) semisweet chocolate chips

1. Heat oven to 375°F. Place sheets of foil on countertop for cooling cookies.

2. Place brown sugar, shortening, water and vanilla in large bowl. Beat at medium speed of electric mixer until well blended. Add eggs; beat well.

3. Combine flour, cocoa, salt and baking soda. Add to shortening mixture; beat at low speed just until blended. Stir in chocolate chips.

4. Drop dough by rounded measuring tablespoonfuls 2 inches apart onto ungreased baking sheet.

5. Bake one baking sheet at a time at 375°F for 7 to 9 minutes or until cookies are set. *Do not overbake.* Cool 2 minutes on baking sheet. Remove cookies to foil to cool completely.

Makes about 3 dozen cookies

Toasted Almond
Brownie Cookies

1 cup blanched whole almonds
1½ cups firmly packed light brown
    sugar
⅔ cup Crisco all-vegetable shortening
    or ⅔ Crisco Stick
1 tablespoon water
1 teaspoon almond extract
2 eggs
1½ cups all-purpose flour
⅓ cup unsweetened cocoa powder
½ teaspoon salt
¼ teaspoon baking soda
2 cups (12 ounces) semisweet
    chocolate chips

1. Heat oven to 350°F. Spread almonds on baking sheet; bake at 350°F for 7 to 10 minutes or until golden brown, stirring several times. Cool. Chop coarsely; reserve.

2. *Increase oven temperature to 375°F.* Place sheets of foil on countertop for cooling cookies.

3. Place brown sugar, shortening, water and almond extract in large bowl. Beat at medium speed of electric mixer until well blended. Add eggs; beat well.

4. Combine flour, cocoa, salt and baking soda. Add to shortening mixture; beat at low speed just until blended. Stir in chocolate chips and reserved almonds.

5. Drop dough by rounded measuring tablespoonfuls 2 inches apart onto ungreased baking sheet.

6. Bake one baking sheet at a time at 375°F for 7 to 9 minutes or until cookies are set. *Do not overbake.* Cool 2 minutes on baking sheet. Remove cookies to foil to cool completely.   *Makes about 3 dozen cookies*

Plan ahead! To have freshly baked cookies ready in minutes, place dough in a tightly covered container and refrigerate up to one week or freeze up to six months. Or, form cookies on baking sheet, freeze and transfer to plastic bag for up to six months. Thaw dough before baking.

CHEWY BROWNIE COOKIES

Chocolate Cheesecake Bars

Brownies

- 1½ cups firmly packed light brown sugar
- ⅔ cup Crisco all-vegetable shortening or ⅔ Crisco Stick
- 1 tablespoon water
- 1 teaspoon vanilla
- 2 eggs
- 1½ cups all-purpose flour
- ⅓ cup unsweetened cocoa powder
- ½ teaspoon salt
- ¼ teaspoon baking soda
- 2 cups (12 ounces) miniature semisweet chocolate chips

Topping

- 1 (8-ounce) *plus* 1 (3-ounce) package cream cheese, softened
- 2 eggs
- ¾ cup granulated sugar
- 1 teaspoon vanilla

1. Heat oven to 350°F. Grease 13 × 9-inch baking pan. Place cooling rack on countertop.

2. For brownies, place brown sugar, shortening, water and vanilla in large bowl. Beat at medium speed of electric mixer until well blended. Add eggs; beat well.

3. Combine flour, cocoa, salt and baking soda. Add to shortening mixture; beat at low speed just until blended. Stir in miniature chocolate chips. Spread dough evenly onto bottom of prepared pan.

4. For topping, place cream cheese, eggs, granulated sugar and vanilla in medium bowl. Beat at medium speed until well blended. Spread evenly over top of brownie mixture.

5. Bake at 350°F for 35 to 40 minutes or until set. *Do not overbake.* Place on cooling rack. Run spatula around edge of pan to loosen. Cool completely on cooling rack. Cut into 2 × 1½-inch bars. Garnish as desired.

Makes about 3 dozen brownies

Almond Mocha Cookie Bars

Cookie Base
1 cup slivered almonds
1½ cups firmly packed light brown sugar
⅔ cup Crisco all-vegetable shortening or ⅔ Crisco Stick
2 tablespoons instant or espresso coffee powder
1 tablespoon cold coffee
1 teaspoon vanilla
½ teaspoon almond extract
2 eggs
1½ cups all-purpose flour
⅓ cup unsweetened cocoa powder
½ teaspoon salt
¼ teaspoon baking soda
1 cup (6 ounces) miniature semisweet chocolate chips

Glaze
1 cup confectioners sugar
1 tablespoon cold coffee
1 tablespoon coffee-flavored liqueur or cold coffee (optional)

1. Heat oven to 350°F. Grease 13 × 9-inch baking pan. Place cooling rack on countertop.

2. For cookie base, spread almonds onto baking sheet; bake at 350°F for 7 to 10 minutes or until golden brown, stirring several times. Cool completely. Chop coarsely.

3. Place brown sugar, shortening, coffee powder, coffee, vanilla and almond extract in large bowl. Beat at medium speed of electric mixer until well blended. Add eggs; beat well.

4. Combine flour, cocoa, salt and baking soda. Add to shortening mixture; beat at low speed just until blended. Stir in small chocolate chips and reserved almonds. Spread mixture evenly into prepared pan.

5. Bake at 350°F for 30 to 35 minutes or until set. *Do not overbake.* Cool completely on wire rack. Cut into 2 × 1½-inch bars.

6. For glaze, combine confectioners sugar, coffee and coffee liqueur, if desired, in small bowl. Stir until well blended. Add additional coffee, a little at a time, if icing is too thick, or add additional confectioners sugar, if icing is too thin. Drizzle glaze over bars.

Makes about 3 dozen bars

German Chocolate Brownie Cookies

Cookies
1½ cups firmly packed light
  brown sugar
⅔ cup Crisco all-vegetable
  shortening or ⅔ Crisco
  Stick
1 tablespoon water
1 teaspoon vanilla
2 eggs
1½ cups all-purpose flour
⅓ cup unsweetened cocoa
  powder
½ teaspoon salt
¼ teaspoon baking soda
2 cups (12 ounces)
  semisweet chocolate
  chips

Topping
½ cup evaporated milk
½ cup granulated sugar
¼ cup Butter Flavor Crisco
  all-vegetable shortening
  or ¼ Butter Flavor
  Crisco Stick*
2 egg yolks, lightly beaten
½ teaspoon vanilla
½ cup chopped pecans
½ cup flaked coconut

*Crisco all-vegetable shortening can be substituted for Butter Flavor Crisco or Butter Flavor Crisco Stick.

1. Heat oven to 375°F. Place sheets of foil on countertop for cooling cookies.

2. For cookies, place brown sugar, shortening, water and vanilla in large bowl. Beat at medium speed of electric mixer until well blended. Add eggs; beat well.

3. Combine flour, cocoa, salt and baking soda. Add to shortening mixture; beat at low speed just until blended. Stir in chocolate chips.

4. Drop dough by rounded measuring tablespoonfuls 2 inches apart onto ungreased baking sheet.

5. Bake one baking sheet at a time at 375°F for 7 to 9 minutes or until cookies are set. *Do not overbake.* Cool 2 minutes on baking sheet. Remove cookies to foil to cool completely.

6. For topping, combine evaporated milk, granulated sugar, shortening and egg yolks in medium saucepan. Stir over medium heat until thickened. Remove from heat. Stir in vanilla, pecans and coconut. Cool completely. Frost cookies.

Makes about 3 dozen cookies

*Top to bottom: Maple Pecan
Sandwich Cookies (page 60),
German Chocolate Brownie Cookies,
Good 'n' Tasties (page 41)*

Caramel Nut Chocolate Cookies

1½ cups firmly packed light brown sugar
⅔ cup Crisco all-vegetable shortening or ⅔ Crisco Stick
1 tablespoon water
1 teaspoon vanilla
2 eggs
1¾ cups all-purpose flour
⅓ cup unsweetened cocoa powder
½ teaspoon salt
¼ teaspoon baking soda
2 cups (12 ounces) miniature semisweet chocolate chips
1 cup chopped pecans
20 to 25 caramels, unwrapped and halved

1. Heat oven to 375°F. Place sheets of foil on countertop for cooling cookies.

2. Place brown sugar, shortening, water and vanilla in large bowl. Beat at medium speed of electric mixer until well blended. Add eggs; beat well.

3. Combine flour, cocoa, salt and baking soda. Add to shortening mixture; beat at low speed just until blended. Stir in miniature chocolate chips.

4. Shape dough into 1¼-inch balls. Dip tops into chopped pecans. Place 2 inches apart on ungreased baking sheet. Press caramel half in center of each ball.

5. Bake one baking sheet at a time at 375°F for 7 to 9 minutes or until cookies are set. *Do not overbake.* Cool 2 minutes on baking sheet. Remove cookies to foil to cool completely.

Makes about 4 dozen cookies

Caramel Nut Chocolate Cookies

Cracked Chocolate Cookies

1½ cups firmly packed light brown sugar
⅔ cup Crisco all-vegetable shortening or ⅔ Crisco Stick
1 tablespoon water
1 teaspoon vanilla
2 eggs
1½ cups all-purpose flour

⅓ cup unsweetened cocoa powder
½ teaspoon salt
¼ teaspoon baking soda
2 cups (12 ounces) miniature semisweet chocolate chips
1 cup confectioners sugar

1. Heat oven to 375°F. Place sheets of foil on countertop for cooling cookies.

2. Place brown sugar, shortening, water and vanilla in large bowl. Beat at medium speed of electric mixer until well blended. Add eggs; beat well.

3. Combine flour, cocoa, salt and baking soda. Add to shortening mixture; beat at low speed just until blended. Stir in miniature chocolate chips.

4. Shape dough into 1¼-inch balls. Roll in confectioners sugar. Place 2 inches apart on ungreased baking sheet.

5. Bake one baking sheet at a time at 375°F for 7 to 9 minutes or until cookies are set. *Do not overbake.* Cool 2 minutes on baking sheet. Remove cookies to foil to cool completely.

Makes about 4 dozen cookies

Chocolate Malted Cookies

¾ cup firmly packed light brown sugar
⅔ cup Crisco all-vegetable shortening or ⅔ Crisco Stick
1 teaspoon vanilla
1 egg
1¾ cups all-purpose flour

½ cup malted milk powder
⅓ cup unsweetened cocoa powder
¾ teaspoon baking soda
½ teaspoon salt
2 cups malted milk balls, broken into large pieces*

*Place malted milk balls in heavy resealable plastic bag; break malted milk balls with rolling pin or back of heavy spoon.

1. Heat oven to 375°F. Place sheets of foil on countertop for cooling cookies.

2. Place brown sugar, shortening and vanilla in large bowl. Beat at medium speed of electric mixer until well blended. Add egg; beat well.

3. Combine flour, malted milk powder, cocoa, baking soda and salt. Add to shortening mixture; beat at low speed just until blended. Stir in malted milk pieces.

4. Drop dough by rounded measuring tablespoonfuls 2 inches apart onto ungreased baking sheet.

5. Bake one baking sheet at a time at 375°F for 7 to 9 minutes or until cookies are set. *Do not overbake.* Cool 2 minutes on baking sheet. Remove cookies to foil to cool completely.

Makes about 3 dozen cookies

Chocolate-Mint Brownie Cookies

1½ cups firmly packed light brown sugar
⅔ cup Crisco all-vegetable shortening or ⅔ Crisco Stick
1 tablespoon water
1 teaspoon vanilla
½ teaspoon peppermint extract

2 eggs
1½ cups all-purpose flour
⅓ cup unsweetened cocoa powder
½ teaspoon salt
¼ teaspoon baking soda
2 cups (12 ounces) mint chocolate chips

1. Heat oven to 375°F. Place sheets of foil on countertop for cooling cookies.

2. Place brown sugar, shortening, water, vanilla and peppermint extract in large bowl. Beat at medium speed of electric mixer until well blended. Add eggs; beat well.

3. Combine flour, cocoa, salt and baking soda. Add to shortening mixture; beat at low speed just until blended. Stir in mint chocolate chips.

4. Drop dough by rounded measuring tablespoonfuls 2 inches apart onto ungreased baking sheet.

5. Bake one baking sheet at a time at 375°F for 7 to 9 minutes or until cookies are set. *Do not overbake.* Cool 2 minutes on baking sheet. Remove cookies to foil to cool completely.

Makes about 3 dozen cookies

White Chocolate Chunk & Macadamia Nut Brownie Cookies

1½ cups firmly packed light brown sugar
⅔ cup Crisco all-vegetable shortening or ⅔ Crisco Stick
1 tablespoon water
1 teaspoon vanilla
2 eggs
1½ cups all-purpose flour
⅓ cup unsweetened cocoa powder
½ teaspoon salt
¼ teaspoon baking soda
1 cup white chocolate chunks or chips
1 cup coarsely chopped macadamia nuts

1. Heat oven to 375°F. Place sheets of foil on countertop for cooling cookies.

2. Place brown sugar, shortening, water and vanilla in large bowl. Beat at medium speed of electric mixer until well blended. Add eggs; beat well.

3. Combine flour, cocoa, salt and baking soda. Add to shortening mixture; beat at low speed just until blended. Stir in white chocolate chunks and macadamia nuts.

4. Drop dough by rounded measuring tablespoonfuls 2 inches apart onto ungreased baking sheet.

5. Bake one baking sheet at a time at 375°F for 7 to 9 minutes or until cookies are set. *Do not overbake.* Cool 2 minutes on baking sheet. Remove cookies to foil to cool completely.

Makes about 3 dozen cookies

INDEX

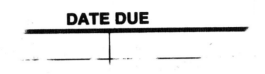

DATE DUE

A FOOTHILLS MEADOW IN BLOOM

GLACIERS ON THE MINARETS

LE CONTE FALLS ON TUOLUMNE RIVER

A FIELD AT TIMBER LINE

SEQUOIAS IN CONGRESS GROVE

MIRROR LAKE

THE GREAT WESTERN DIVIDE FROM ABOVE THE MIDDLE FORK OF THE KAWEAH RIVER

TIME
LIFE
BOOKS ®

THE HIGH SIERRA

THE AMERICAN WILDERNESS / TIME-LIFE BOOKS / NEW YORK

BY EZRA BOWEN
AND THE EDITORS OF TIME-LIFE BOOKS

THE AMERICAN WILDERNESS
Series Editor: Charles Osborne

Editorial Staff for The High Sierra:
Picture Editor: Susan Rayfield
Designer: Charles Mikolaycak
Staff Writers: Gerald Simons,
Betsy Frankel
Chief Researcher: Martha T. Goolrick
Researchers: Terry Drucker,
Margo Dryden, Susanna Seymour,
Timberlake Wertenbaker
Design Assistant: Mervyn Clay

Editorial Production
Production Editor: Douglas B. Graham
Quality Director: Robert L. Young
Assistant: James J. Cox
Copy Staff: Rosalind Stubenberg,
Eleanore W. Karsten, Florence Keith
Picture Department: Dolores A. Littles,
Joan Lynch

Valuable assistance was given by the following departments and individuals of Time Inc.: Editorial Production, Norman Airey, Margaret T. Fischer; Library, Peter Draz; Picture Collection, Doris O'Neil; Photographic Laboratory, George Karas; TIME-LIFE News Service, Murray J. Gart; Correspondent Pat Tucker (Washington, D.C.).

The Author: Ezra Bowen is an editor on the staff of TIME-LIFE BOOKS. A native of the East, he has spent considerable time in the West—including the wilderness of the Sierra Nevada. Mr. Bowen began his writing career as a reporter for *Newsweek.* He later served for 10 years as a writer and senior editor for SPORTS ILLUSTRATED. He joined TIME-LIFE BOOKS as Director of Educational Research and Development in 1964, then resumed his writing in late 1965. Since then he has co-authored the LIFE Science Library's *Wheels,* written the *Middle Atlantic States* volume of the TIME-LIFE Library of America and edited the TIME-LIFE series This Fabulous Century.

The Consultant: Martin Litton, who was born in California, made his first trip into the Sierra at 16—with one other boy and a donkey to carry their gear. Since then he has walked most of the high wild parts of the range. Following World War II service as an Army Air Force pilot, Litton wrote features about the outdoors for the *Los Angeles Times,* and later joined *Sunset* magazine. Since leaving the magazine in 1969, Litton, who is a director of the Sierra Club, has been a freelance photographer and writer on the wilderness.

The Cover: One of several unnamed lakes grouped together at 11,000 feet in Upper Pioneer Basin (part of the John Muir Wilderness) reflects the setting sun. Mount Mills (13,468 feet) rises above the snow field at center, and Mount Abbot (13,715 feet) is at left.

Contents

The Setting of the Sierra

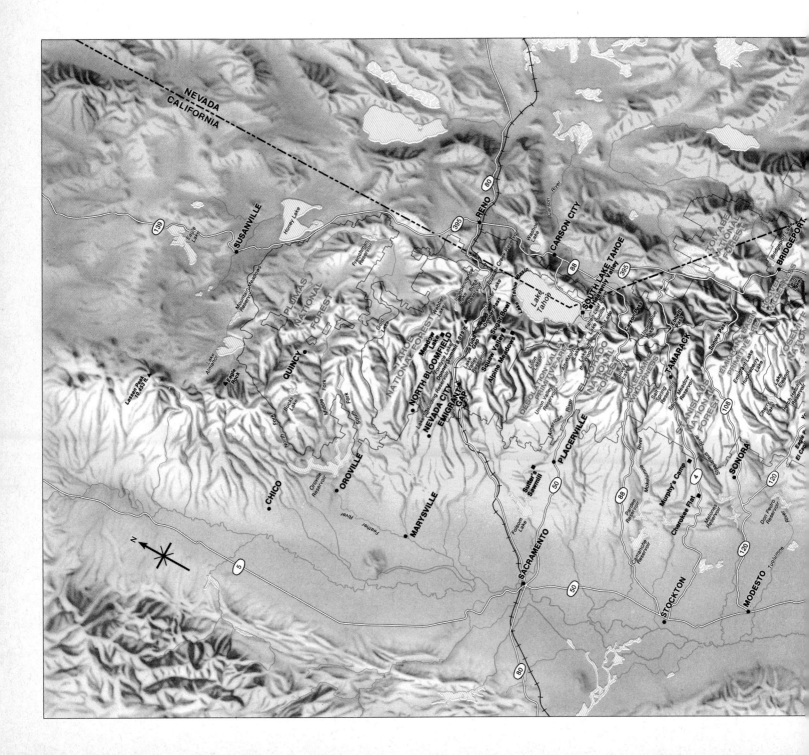

The Sierra Nevada region, covering an enormous section of California and a small corner of Nevada (shaded area at right), is mapped below, highlighting the features discussed in this book. The mountain terrain of the high Sierra appears in yellow, with surrounding foothills and lowlands shown in green. Red outlines enclose tracts of federally protected land: national parks, national forests, primitive areas and sections set aside permanently by the Wilderness Act of 1964. Lakes and rivers are portrayed in blue; lake beds that contain water only part of the year appear here as mottled blue areas surrounded by broken lines. Black triangles mark major peaks, round dots towns and cities. Squares denote points of scenic, recreational or historic interest. Otherwise, standard map symbols are used. Trails are shown by black lines, paved roads by double lines, railroads by lines with crossbars.

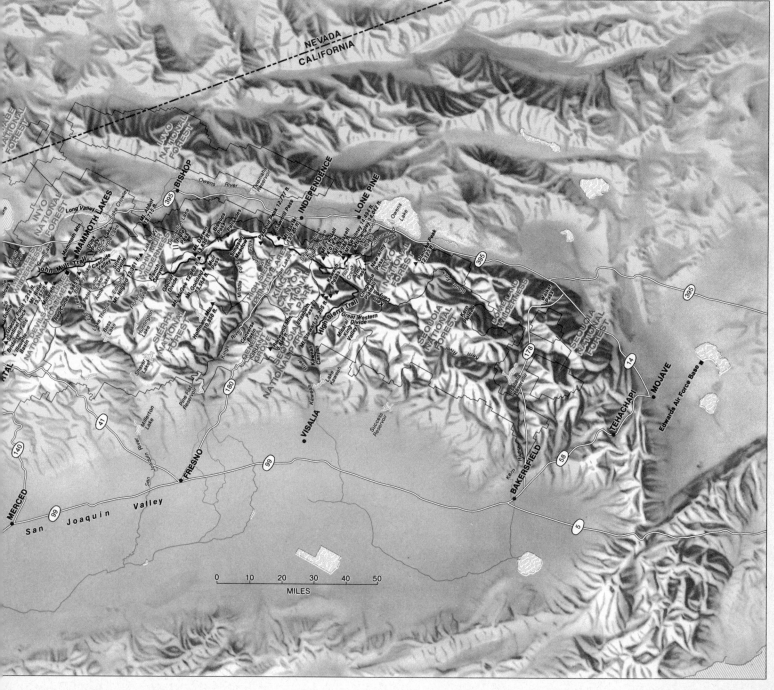

1/ The Air the Angels Breathe

*These beautiful days must enrich all my life. They do
not exist as mere pictures ... but they saturate themselves
into every part of the body and live always.*

JOHN MUIR/ *MY FIRST WINTER IN THE YOSEMITE VALLEY*

On an Indian summer morning three horsemen turn a string of pack
mules onto a trail that climbs among the conifers and tumbled granite
at the head of Cottonwood Canyon, high on the eastern rim of the Sierra Nevada wilderness, about 260 miles southeast of San Francisco.
The October sun is hard and white; there is no cloud nor even a hint of
morning dew upon the air. Each thud of a hoof sends up a tiny explosion of granite dust to settle onto the leaves of trailside shrubs or to
sift upward into the nostrils and throats of the riders, who are breathing deeply and thirstily in the unaccustomed thinness of the atmosphere
above 10,000 feet.

There was a light freeze along the trail here last night, and in a patch
of alpine meadow dampened by the seepage from Cottonwood Creek
the mud is puckered by frost boils. In one north-facing copse, where
the porous soil holds the hoofprints of mule deer, frost crystals gleam
on the sedge and shriveled ruins of shooting-star blossoms sag on their
stems. Ahead a fat marmot, already drowsy from the impulse to hibernate, whistles his disapproval at the approaching horses, and then
waddles slowly into his rock burrow.

Somewhat like the marmot, the horsemen are adjusting to a change
in their environment; but to them the transition has been sudden and
not a little disorienting. Only two hours earlier they were 7,000 feet
lower, in the heavier air and desert heat of the Owens Valley—still in

sight to the east of the trail they are riding. The quick gain in altitude has left them feeling dehydrated, vaguely headachy and more enervated than they would like to be in the first hour of a week-long ride into the high country. Moreover the morning sun has not yet burned off the last of the night's chill, and the riders turn up the collars of sheepskin and canvas jackets as a wind comes tumbling down Cottonwood Canyon. Mark Twain, who roughed it through the Sierra much in the manner of these horse-borne campers, was himself often discommoded by the numbing drops in temperature bred by the mountain winds. "I have seen a perfectly blistering morning open up with the thermometer at ninety degrees at eight o'clock," he once commented, "and seen the snow fall fourteen inches deep. . . . There are only two seasons in the region . . . the breaking up of one winter and the beginning of the next . . . it snows at least once in every single month."

It still does. In the warm week before a recent Labor Day, a mother whose two youngsters were sleeping outdoors below timber line awoke to a commotion outside her cabin. She looked out onto ground covered by new snow; the kids were shouting, groaning, shaking the snow off their sleeping bags and trying to slap and finger-comb the matted ice from their hair. In July of 1941 at old Army Pass, just around an ice-cracked cliff from the Cottonwood trail, a party of hikers spent an hour and a half hacking a stairway out of the wall of snow that still buried the easy horse trail to the pass. And in 1968 the snow was so deep through the summer that the old trail was virtually abandoned for a newer route up a warmer south-facing headwall.

Turning now toward this new route the packstring ambles across a meadow that embraces a chain of ponds called, rather grandly, Cottonwood Lakes. One of the riders dismounts to ease the agony of city-soft muscles congealed in the unfamiliar contours of a Western saddle and to take a drink from a lake. The water is sweet and pure, but no more so than the air, which has been warming in the late-morning sun and now caresses the meadow in a movement that is no longer a wind, only a stirring. Here beneath the summit peaks is a sharpness of light that seems to surround everything, bringing out each subtle texture and color tone. And the air is so clean that every leaf and stone and flake of bark and blade of grass is sharply delineated, every shadow drawn as with a needle. Mark Twain took note of this, too: "The air up there . . . is very pure and fine, bracing and delicious," he wrote. "And why shouldn't it be?—it is the same the angels breathe."

The horsemen begin the last climb to the crest of the pass, over a rough, narrow set of switchbacks that zigzag for some 800 vertical feet across a fall of boulders and sharp-edged talus. At the highest, most tenuous spot near the top a rider dismounts to unhitch the lead ropes that have secured one animal to the next. Two mules fell here not long ago, down into the rocks; and there is no desire now to repeat the performance, with perhaps the whole packstring being peeled off the trail like a rope of rock-climbers being snatched from a precipice by one falling comrade. Abruptly, the horses top the final rise. And there, in a great arc from north to west, is the wild, austere sweep of the High Sierra heartland.

Wave upon wave of rock has been heaved and tossed and eroded here into the most dramatic stretch of wilderness anywhere in the old continental United States. At every point in the arc the eye is overwhelmed by the immensity of rock, the presence of rock, the height, the shape and the enormous power of rock that dominates this land. Across the first saddle, a bare beige dip of weathered stone, is 14,042-foot Mount Langley, its flattish crown notched from the tumbling out of granite blocks split off by the brutal action of winter frost. From Langley the other crags of the Sierra crest rise in terrible sawteeth to the summit of 14,494-foot Mount Whitney, climax of the Sierra wilderness and the tallest mountain in the old 48 states. To the west the brown barrens sweep down to the timber above Rock Creek. Then the land sinks into the ruler-straight trough of Kern Canyon, rises onto the gravelly, pine-wooded terrace of Chagoopa Plateau to climax once more in the red and black spires of the Kaweah Peaks—the tallest nearly 14,000 feet and molded in relief by smoke from a lowland forest fire.

Within sight of these mountains are a half dozen others soaring above 14,000 feet. And off beyond the horizon to the north stands a ragged rank of some 500 peaks above 12,000 feet, their crowns laced with mini-glaciers and crescents of lingering snow. Along the line of mountains the heights are slashed from east to west by glacial gorges whose granite walls plunge farther than those of any other canyons in North America: at the foot of Junction Ridge, where the South and Middle Forks of the Kings River come brawling together, the defile drops 8,200 feet to the stream bed, deeper by 2,000 feet than the Grand Canyon.

Ninety-five miles to the north, past the pumice-strewn cone of Mammoth Mountain and the dark volcanic spires of the Minarets, is the bold drama of the Yosemite, whose precipices rise even more abruptly

than those of Kings Canyon, though not so high. Here the Merced River is born in a moonscape of granite where little will grow but lichen and moss and mattings of stunted whitebark pine. Here, too, as in the bowl by the Cottonwood Lakes and all through the high country, the rock is so hard, so enduring that in many places even the grinding force of the glaciers could not disturb it. Instead the moving ice could only scour and polish so that in a certain slant of sun whole mountainsides shine too brightly for the eye to endure for more than a few seconds at a time. Below these mirrors of stone the tributaries of the Merced meet in an abyss of granite. Farther down, the riverbanks, looping through a meadow some seven miles long, are guarded by tall ponderosa pine and sweetened by the fragrance of incense cedar. Nowhere in the world is a more beautiful valley than this, flanked by walls of monolithic rock that rise on either side from 3,000 to 4,800 feet above the meadow—El Capitan, Glacier Point, Sentinel Rock, Half Dome—laced with half a dozen waterfalls: the highest, Yosemite, tumbles and free-falls 2,565 feet (Niagara is only 167 feet) to join the Merced.

Yet throughout the Sierra there are other sights just as captivating, though perhaps more fleeting and subtler. On the western edge of the range the foothills take a slow upward rise from the San Joaquin Valley. Then beginning at Visalia, 75 miles south of Fresno, the land rolls and pitches 45 miles eastward through a series of powerful folds to the heights of the Great Western Divide. The average gradient on this western slope is only 6 per cent—about 300 feet to the mile. Yet as a traveler gradually gains altitude he becomes aware of a steady drop in the temperature and a corresponding change in the whole look of the land as he moves upward from the subtropical heat of the valley to the relative chill among the peaks. In certain places, particularly along the steeper river courses, this climatic shift is so pronounced that on a recent December morning inside the canyon of the Middle Fork of the Kaweah River a single sweep of the eye could take in a weather show that might have unfolded from Florida to Alaska.

Down on the river bottom, where the altitude is no more than 800 feet above sea level, a thunderstorm was moving across grassy hillocks and stands of sycamore trees. At 1,700 feet a camper, comfortable in a light sweater, stood at the edge of a field of live oak and tarweed, spattered by random drops of temperate rain. On the north side of the canyon a tall rock dotted by maples was in fog, dank at the cloud bottom, a hint of chill rolling down the slope. Across the canyon another higher peak was dusted by snow that grew visibly deeper until the mountain

In their precision and symmetry, the gray basalt shafts above—part of the Devils Postpile in the central Sierra —look as if they had been carved in a sculptor's studio. Actually the obelisks were formed some four million years ago when a deep pool of lava, cooling and shrinking, developed vertical cracks; subsequent erosion and glacial action exposed the pillars. Such basaltic outcroppings are common, but this symmetry of cracking is found in few other similar formations.

disappeared into its own cloud covering. And in a burst of sunlight at the head of the gorge shone the massif of Mount Stewart, its glacier buried beneath a blanket of wind-crusted snow.

Blended into the setting for this climatic spectrum stands an extravagant race of trees, native only to the moist western slope of the Sierra. And a man moving into the wilderness comes upon them almost by chance as the way climbs up the northern edge of Kaweah Canyon. Suddenly, set back in the forest will be a tree trunk perhaps 14 feet across. The massive shaft, its cinnamon-red bark fluted like a Grecian column, rises bare of branches for perhaps 90 feet to disappear into the canopy of white fir and sugar pine clustered in attendance about its waist. Above those lesser trees, themselves more than 100 feet tall, the great creature crowns at a height of 200 feet or more. Botanists classify these trees as *Sequoiadendron giganteum;* old Sierra hands know them, more humbly, as the Big Trees. Either name is correct. For the sequoias are the largest living things on earth. And this first giant is, like Small Porgies in Kipling's *Just So* story of the colossal creatures that live on the sea bottom, one of the younger, smaller members of the family.

There are 3,500 more here in a single grove called Giant Forest, with another 13,000 in scattered stands nearby and north to Yosemite and beyond. Everything about them is on a heroic scale, so much so that a first-time visitor tends to lose any sense of proportion and must stand among them awhile to absorb their true size. In any mature grove the most ordinary are 20 feet in diameter; and the very largest measure 35 to 40 feet through—enough to block a city street from curb to curb. Their bark is as much as two feet thick and deeply scarred by ground fires that raced through the forest in years past, cleaning out the lesser growth and leaving black gnawings among the root buttresses of the Big Trees. The branches, where they begin to occur high overhead, are heavy, twisted, bullish, ungraceful, yet they taper into smoke puffs of evergreen leaves as delicate as those of a young cedar, with tiny cones no bigger than a baby's fist. No one knows when these regal monsters first germinated, but probably they have been growing for 3,500 years or more. A few are over 300 feet tall, though the tops of many older trees have been blasted off by lightning as they reared above the surrounding forest centuries ago. The smell that fills these groves is the rich, dry scent of ripe redwood shavings. And the sound of the wind in the sequoias' crowns is high and soft and distant, like the rush of a cataract far off, a sound of prehistory, agonizingly pure and haunting, a sigh from a lost time when there were no men here.

It is, in all, a land of primeval grandeur, this high Sierra; of granite crags striated by avalanche gullies; of trees tortured and dwarfed at timber line but superbly tall in the forests below; of scores of booming cascades and nearly 2,000 mountain lakes and ponds, each resting in its cup of granite or of flower-speckled meadow grass. It is a land that has remained in many ways as wild as it was 200 years ago when the Spanish missionary Fray Pedro Font first spied its gleaming peaks from the west and named it *una gran sierra nevada* (a great snowy range). It is a land still browsed by bands of bighorn sheep and mule deer, a land prowled by the mountain lion and the pine marten and watched over by the lordly golden eagle.

That this high country has survived so well as wilderness is due very much to its formidable geology. For the Sierra splits the state of California for 400 longitudinal miles from just below Lassen Peak in the north down to the petering out into cactus flats near the town of Mojave in the south. From the earliest days of exploration these mountains, which rise at Whitney to a wall standing two full miles above the valley, have been a redoubtable barrier to any white man who felt he had to enter them (the Indians, more sensible about such things, rarely bothered, except for the urgent business of trade or hunting or war—and then only in the best days of summer).

John Charles Frémont, the celebrated trailblazer, political adventurer and gold speculator, reduced an aged Indian to tears of commiseration by asking in the bleak January of 1844 just how a man might cross these ridges at the gentler elevations southwest of Lake Tahoe. The trail was very hard, replied the Indian—six sleeps in summer, and in winter one should not go at all: "Rock on rock, snow on snow," he chanted, "and even if you get over the snow you will not be able to get down from the mountain." Frémont went nonetheless, and did manage to make it over the snow and down the mountain, but not until he had been so thoroughly blizzard-bound and starved that his party had to slaughter and eat virtually everything on four legs, including their pet dog Tlamath. It was three years later and barely 40 miles away that a party of emigrants, led by an injudicious man named George Donner, found itself even more hard pressed and resorted to more bizarre fare: "Mrs. Murphy said here yesterday," noted one diary, "that she thought she would commence on Milton and eat him, I do not think she has done so yet, it is so distressing. . . ."

Though the menu for visitors has improved, these mountains are not

always easy to cross even today. From Pyramid Peak, where the 10,000-foot-elevations of the true high country begin just below Donner Pass, to the edge of the Kern Plateau south of Whitney, only five winding paved roads have been cut through, and four of those are snowed shut from November to May or June. There is one stretch of 160 crow-flight miles running north from the Kern country to Tuolumne Meadows on the eastern edge of Yosemite with no roads at all, only footpaths and horse trails twisting up to passes hacked out of the granite at altitudes up to 13,600 feet.

It has taken more than an accident of geology, however, to keep this wilderness from vanishing under the sooty blanket of civilization. California, with 20 million people in 1970, is the most populous state and one of the fastest growing. Each year over a fourth of the population, reinforced by armies of out-of-staters, crowds into the Sierra to sightsee or go camping. And of these, perhaps two million tread on some corner of the real high country.

Yet, with some woeful exceptions, that tread has remained comparatively light. For in acts of wisdom and foresight rare in an ambitious, basically exploitative people, the high Sierra has been placed in the protective embrace of eight national forests and three enormous national parks, Yosemite—which is bigger than the state of Rhode Island—and the contiguous Sequoia and Kings Canyon Parks, together even larger and the major seedbed for the Big Trees. Certain enclaves along the rivers have been given over to the lowland cities for reservoirs; limited sections are open either to supervised timber cutting, livestock grazing or the operation of tourist facilities—all of which infuriate the lovers of primitive land. But most of the Sierra back country is essentially wild. And there are some 939,000 acres within the national forests that have been designated by Congress under the Wilderness Act of 1964 to be preserved as Wilderness with a capital "W," a place where man may come only as a visitor and leave the land exactly as he finds it—in the natural state of things. In addition almost 1.4 million acres of the high country in the parks, where timbering and even hunting have always been prohibited, have been put under study for possible inclusion as legalized Wilderness.

The Wilderness Act was a sweet triumph in a foot-slogging hundred years' war by American conservationists, who won their first important skirmish right here in the Sierra. So far the new bill has guaranteed the preservation for all time of 10.1 million wild acres and prodded Con-

gress to start reviewing another 56.2 million acres for possible Wilderness designation. In folding such land under its wing, the act formally defines a Wilderness as an area "retaining its primeval character and influence, without permanent improvements or human habitation and which generally appears to have been affected primarily by the forces of nature, with the imprint of man's work substantially unnoticeable [and which] has outstanding opportunities for solitude or a primitive and unconfined type of recreation." The act also contains a statement of policy, a sort of preamble, whose basic message marks the end point of nearly 400 years in the evolution of attitudes toward the role of wilderness in American society: "It is hereby declared to be the policy of the Congress to secure for the American people of present and future generations the benefits of an enduring resource of wilderness. For this purpose there is hereby established a National Wilderness Preservation System to be composed of federally owned areas . . . administered for the use and enjoyment of the American people . . . and so as to provide for the protection of these areas, the preservation of their wilderness character. . . ."

That is not the way either the government or much of its constituency has historically looked upon the wilderness. The reaction of the first European settlers was pure revulsion. Governor William Bradford of the Plymouth Colony wrote gloomily in the 1630s that in his domain ". . . the whole country, full of woods and thickets, represented a wild and savage hue." And his heart was wholly with the Pilgrims, who had landed only a decade before: ". . . what could they see but a hideous and desolate wilderness, full of wild beasts and wild men . . . for which way soever they turned their eyes (save upward to the heavens) they could have little solace or content in respect of any outward objects." More than 200 years later the spiritual value of wilderness was still beyond the popular line of sight. A shepherd, stuck with his herd for the summer grazing season in a godforsaken gorge called Yosemite, in 1869, grumbled: "There is nothing worth seeing anywhere, only rocks, and I see plenty of them here."

The more common reflex, that of the real American he-man upon being confronted with such wild vistas, was to shoot anything that moved, chop down anything that grew, and salivate over the profits to be grubbed from the primeval soil. By 1850, following a series of gold strikes among the Sierra foothills and neighboring ranges, 100,000 men had come scrambling in, dredging and damming streams, killing Indians and each other, and generally making a mess of whatever they

touched. After the discovery of silver in 1859 on the Nevada side of the Sierra—from the supposedly "illimitable" timber supply of "colossal specimens of yellow, sugar, pitch and fir pines" on the western slope —some 600 million board feet were whacked out as shoring for silver-mine tunnels alone. As the land opened up, livestock drovers grazed some three million head of cattle and nearly six million sheep through the mountains, stripping the high meadows. Meat hunters decimated the wild bands of bighorn sheep, deer, elk and antelope; and any dangerous (i.e., competitive) predators such as wolves or grizzly bears were pushed well down the road toward total extinction under the banner of civilization. "It was deemed enough," wrote one Californian, "if the trails could be made safe for the children to go to school, and if a reasonable proportion of the stock survived the Indians and wild animals."

But even then a few quiet voices were beginning to suggest that there was more to be had from a wilderness than targets and treasure. Emerson said, "In the wilderness, I find something more dear and connate than in the streets or villages . . . in the woods we return to reason and faith." And a Massachusetts poet and lover of the ways of wild things, Henry David Thoreau, was asking a persistent and practical question: "Why should not we . . . have our national preserves . . . in which the bear and panther, and some even of the hunter race, may still exist, and not be 'civilized off the face of the earth'—our forests . . . not for idle sport or food, but for inspiration and our own true recreation?"

Incredibly for those rapacious times a few powerful men listened to such voices; and in 1864 Congress passed a bill ceding Yosemite Valley to the state of California as a park, the first such wild preserve to be set aside by federal action anywhere in America, "for public use, resort and recreation." One of the park's early visitors was the youthful John Muir, a Scotsman who arrived leading a band of 2,050 hungry sheep but stayed on to become a devout conservationist and tireless chronicler of the natural wonders of the Sierra.

With Emerson and Thoreau, Muir believed that in wilderness lay truth and man's salvation ("Climb the mountains and get their good tidings. Nature's peace will flow into you as sunshine flows into trees. The winds will blow their own freshness into you, and the storms their energy, while cares will drop off like autumn leaves"). This messianic spirit shines from Muir's surviving portraits; his bearded face seems always in repose, with a soft light of almost celestial understanding showing in the eye—the most parfit gentil naturalist. Yet he was an awesomely energetic man whose passion for his beloved Sierra led him to

such eccentricities as shinnying to the top of a 100-foot pine in the teeth of a gale to be closer to the song of the wind in the needles, and bounding from the door of his cabin during a cataclysmic wrench of the Sierra bedrock, shouting joyously, "A noble earthquake, a noble earthquake!"

Muir would disappear into the high country for days at a time, fortified by a crust of bread and his conviction that nothing truly bad could ever happen in the mountains. The notes gathered on these forays, and later published, were scientifically perceptive and persuasive as conservation propaganda, though the phrases ranged in quality from the sweetest poesy to the most effusive 19th Century goo ("happy mountain raindrops . . . kissing the lips of lilies!"). He was the first to record the existence of living glaciers in the Sierra and to deduce the true effect of ancient ice upon the contours of Yosemite; he compiled detailed observations on the Sierra's creatures and its trees, particularly the sugar pines, which he worshipfully described as the "priests of the pines"; he rhapsodized upon storms and meadows and waterfalls; and he was endlessly fascinated by a peculiar bird called the water ouzel, which has the odd habit of flying under water and walking about on the bottoms of pools, emitting bubbles from its nose.

Muir's preachments upon the Sierra and the need to preserve its wilderness caught the conservationist ear of Teddy Roosevelt, and Muir became a prime mover in the expansion of Yosemite as a public preserve and the transfer of the valley back to federal jurisdiction. Muir originated the idea for another major park named Sequoia, now jointly administered with the adjacent Kings Canyon National Park. He helped prepare the soil in which the seeds of both the National Park and National Forest Services were planted; and by the time of his death in 1914, he had become a kind of spiritual monument to the whole conservation movement, the deep and secret self-image of everyone who would go up into the hills with a pack on his back and an eye on the shining rock of the Sierra crest.

However, Muir and company might be a trifle stunned at a few other consequences of their crusade and would unquestionably have trouble recognizing various of their disciples. The seven million and more who come to the Sierra in peak years arrive in scores of different guises and with just as many different motives. At Yosemite, which trembles under the impact of nearly half the Sierra's total visitors, 90 per cent are auto-borne sightseers who arrive in street shoes to stay for 27 to 44 hours in the franchised motels or the wooden-floored tent communi-

ties; they snap a few pictures, perhaps try a guided trail ride from the dude stables, or buy a four-dollar load of precut wood to toss onto the bonfire at a community sing. Rarely do they venture far from the parking lots or pause long enough to let the Sierra tell them anything. One recent summer's day a woman pressing through Yosemite at a full tourist's gallop was heard to snarl at her husband, "Now I don't want to hear NOTHIN' about flora, fauna or geology, understand?"

This is not precisely what the founding fathers of the wilderness concept had in mind. Neither is the bustle at Sequoia and Kings Canyon, where an annual mass of as many as 1.9 million or more crunch elbows for a quick look at the Big Trees. The crowd brings its drug and money problems and leaves its exhaust smoke and litter behind; a federal judge at park headquarters levies fines and issues sentences for speeding, writing rubber checks, smoking pot and defacing trees.

Yet Yosemite Valley and the beaten-down portals at Sequoia and Kings Canyon represent no more than 21 square miles in a parkland total of 2,503, most of it high wilderness opening directly onto the roadless sweep of the Sierra's back country. Right at the edge of Yosemite Valley a pathway called the John Muir Trail takes off into the heart of the mountains and rambles southward for 212 miles to terminate atop Mount Whitney, never touching pavement and never dropping below 7,500 feet once it leaves the Yosemite area. At Wallace Creek near Mount Whitney the Muir Trail connects with the High Sierra Trail, another wild route, leading 80 miles to Giant Forest. Radiating from these two arteries is a loose pattern of 3,000 more miles of horse and footpaths. In recent years no fewer than 500,000 high-country campers —backpackers and horsemen—have set out upon them to fish the clear lakes, to walk among the wild flowers of summer meadows, to sleep in tents or in sleeping bags beneath the stars, restoring themselves by living for a night or a full summer as part of the wild land.

Not all of them do so with grace. The number of wilderness users has been going up over the long run 10 to 20 per cent a year, so that a few parts of even the high country are in danger of being trampled into a sylvan slum by the very people who have come there to love it. "We're first in the nation in the number of campers," says a national forest supervisor, with a mixture of pride and dismay. Each year the staff of the national parks, assisted by volunteers, haul out some 10 tons of trash from the back-country districts. The Forest and Park Service people also have to mount about 200 search or rescue operations, most of them overnight, for lost or strayed or injured campers. Often a person

disabled on the trail will have to be brought down in a helicopter or on a ranger's horse, most commonly with a sprained ankle or an attack of the giddiness and nausea that can come from exertion at high altitude.

"Today," explains one Yosemite ranger, "a guy with a Sears, Roebuck card can, with a stroke of his pen, buy a complete camper outfit and come up here. He doesn't have the faintest idea of how to use that equipment, or what he's doing. And yet he's just as much of a camper as John Muir, and has every bit as much right to use the wilderness."

The Sierra makes no such allowances. Occasionally the mountains will lash out and take a life when someone is inexperienced or really careless in the high country. Not long ago a woman, a newcomer to the wilderness, tried to cool her feet in a stream that was booming with the snow melt of June. She was swept away and her husband went in to save her. By the wildest luck she caught a rock downstream and pulled herself out; but her husband's body was never found.

Though the lethal potential is always there, the high Sierra is most often kind to its pilgrims, particularly those who treat it with care. And most people do. The typical back-country camper, according to a survey distributed by the Department of Agriculture, is someone used to the wilderness and its ways, someone who has been there before and will go again, with his family or three or four close friends. In the Sierra today there is at least an 80 per cent chance that he is a backpacker; two decades ago "75 to 80 per cent were on horses," says a Forest Service official. "But today you've got a generation that hasn't been brought up around horses; they're not used to them, scared of them, maybe. And I think, too, it has to do with this desire of people to be completely free, independent, not tied to the packstring or anything."

The back-country visitor will stay out for five or six days. And whether on horse or foot he will be there basically to do as John Muir did—to let the beautiful days enrich his life and saturate themselves into every part of the body. He is someone quite like the fireman from Alhambra, California, who went onto the Muir Trail recently with his two sons, aged 11 and 13, to make a very special, very sentimental journey: he had done the Muir once before in 1937 at the age of 12, and now there was the precious dividend of seeing it again through eyes so young.

Or like the slim youngster coming down the Echo Lake trail one morning not long ago, holding hands with a pretty, blissfully happy little brunette. "We're part of a survival class from Berkeley," said the boy, shifting the weight of his backpack. Rarely have two people survived

more successfully than this pair, who had health blooming from every visible piece of skin and all their emergency rations intact after four days out. They had been living on trout caught on bent pins, then roasted on a stick and spiced with algae common to the local lakes. "We read about it in a book," bubbled the girl, "and it was real great."

Such high-country devotees show a remarkably similar attachment to the Sierra, a kind of mystical devotion that takes some time to germinate. For the heartland of this wilderness is, upon first view, not only dramatic but harsh and bare and somewhat forbidding. "You have to let it soak in before you understand this Sierra mystique, what it is," says a Sequoia Park ranger who has spent his life in the mountains. "There's a starkness to this high granite country; you realize that the plants and animals are right on the margin of existence, and hanging on. And," he adds, "you can't help but marvel at it."

Every Sierra lover seems to share this compulsion to explain the special lure of his wilderness so that others will know and understand it and love it as he loves it. But in his heart he does not want any new people to go there or to bring their friends. Because like most passions the love of wilderness tends to be a selfish and a self-centered thing. And every new person is another set of footprints on a trail, another ring of blackened campfire rocks, another flash of a red backpack or an orange tent on a trail or by a lake that the Sierra lover wants for his very own, on that hour of that day, and preferably forever. For this is his Sierra. He wants it just for himself or to share with his closest companions, to see, to use, to savor, to be part of in his own way. Almost any other human appears to him an intruder.

As one of those horsemen on the Cottonwood trail in Indian summer, I can tell you for certain that it is my Sierra. And I tell you, very selfishly, this: I wish no one had ever been here before.

I wish I had been the first man ever to crest New Army Pass and see that wild sweep of Sierra, the first to have heard the wind in the crown of a giant sequoia, the first to have tasted the sweet water in the pools below the falls at Yosemite. But since that cannot be, I will tell you how I like my Sierra now. I like it from horseback. And I like it in the fall when you and all your friends have gone, when the nights are frost-cold and the days warm, the bright gold of aspen leaves backlit by a slant of equinoctial sun. I like it, perhaps most of all, as it was on the afternoon following the ride up from Cottonwood Canyon.

At 4:30 in the afternoon a cold wind was blowing down from the sum-

mit of Mount Whitney, across the wooded meadow where we had made camp. Two of us resaddled our horses and rode up to a lake that lies in the enormous granite bowl below the west face of Whitney. A doe herded her pair of almost identical fawns along the trail ahead of us for a time and then turned them into a copse of willow to stand perfectly still, watching us as we rode by. Around a nose of rock the headwall of the mountain came into view, far above timber, gullied and slashed by avalanche tracks. To its left was the pinnacle of Mount Russell, one of the last major peaks in the Sierra to be climbed—and the taker of one climber's life in 1947. To the right was a palisade whose flanks, like Whitney's, were scored by avalanches. And this same palisade extended around the sky in an unbroken ridge, curving up from the south to embrace Whitney's summit, then around toward Russell and finally tapering down close to the trail on our left.

The sun was lowering toward the Kaweah Peaks when our horses pulled down their heads to drink at the edge of the lake, and the sundown wind was becoming colder and stronger. We dismounted, turned up our coat collars and left the animals, to walk among the stones and boulders. The lake's feeder stream was dried to a bare trickle, but in years past it has been so filled with spawning trout that their backs stood out of water. As we watched the play of wind upon the lake, the sun impaled itself upon the Kaweahs and the refracted light deepened the relief of every crevice, every pinnacle. The last rays combed through yellowing willows and shone dazzling on the polished granite. As the sunset shadow moved up to envelop the lesser heights, only the crown of Whitney was left in sun. And over the space of 15 minutes that crown turned from a luminescent yellow white to burnt orange to the magic lavender of alpenglow, and abruptly to the forbidding slate gray of evening. Then we turned to remount for the ride down, and there appeared by a horse's hoof the perfect counterpoint to all this grandeur, a tiny blue flower—whorled penstemon—no more than two inches above the ground, as small and delicate as the mountains were stark and overpowering. It was a perfect sunset in the Sierra, and the sky was a smear of stars as we unsaddled our horses back at the campground and turned them out to graze for the night.

The Age of John Muir

In 1901, the outdoorsmen of the Sierra Club planned their first camping trip through the high country. Female members received detailed advice: "Skirts can be short, not more than half way from knee to ankle, and under them can be worn shorter dark-colored bloomers. . . . For the women who ride horseback, divided skirts are recommended."

The 21-day expedition delighted John Muir (opposite), president of the Sierra Club since its founding in 1892. The outing also pointed up the tremendous changes that had taken place in Muir's beloved Sierra in his own lifetime. Until the late 1840s, when Muir was brought to America as an 11-year-old Scottish immigrant, the range was a fearsome barrier, little known and seldom penetrated by white men. By the 1860s, when Muir came to live in Yosemite Valley, the Sierra was being mapped and exploited. Now, in 1901, the mountains were judged safe enough for female Sierra Clubbers, who were confidently expected to hike up to 20 miles a day.

These dramatic changes had been set in motion by the discovery of gold on the American River in 1848.

Ragtag hordes of prospectors, followed by mining companies, worked their way upstream from the Sierra foothills. The crude mining camps swelled into raucous boomtowns served by railroads. By 1870, with comfortable trains giving access to the wild interior, tourists were arriving in ever-increasing numbers to marvel at the scenery.

But the landscape, even then, was being violated. Loggers left great fields of stumps. Mining companies diverted rivers and leveled whole hills. Mountain meadows were overgrazed by sheep—"hoofed locusts," Muir called them—that crowded out the wild creatures.

The exploiters got no quarter from John Muir. His antisheep broadsides were largely responsible for the two acts of Congress in 1890 and 1906 that created Yosemite National Park, As late as 1913, just a year before his death, Muir led a campaign against plans to build a reservoir in Hetch Hetchy Valley. He lost that last fight, but Muir's lifework left broad expanses of unspoiled Sierra wilderness, virginal places that proved the wisdom of his creed: "Everyone needs beauty as well as bread."

Naturalist John Muir, 70 years old and still going strong, pauses in Yosemite in 1908 to scan his well-loved mountains. His nature studies took him as far as Alaska, Russia, India and Australia, but he always returned to the Sierra, his spiritual home.

Rich Gold Strikes
and Hungry Prospectors

The early days of the Gold Rush produced a bumper crop of wondrous success stories, some of them true. For 11 days in a row, four miners averaged $1,250 a day working a claim only six feet by 10 feet. Others unearthed supernuggets of pure gold, each weighing 20 pounds or more, and many panned enough gold dust, at $18 an ounce, to shower touring dancers with bags worth a small fortune. But most freelance prospectors had trouble making ends meet at inflated gold-camp prices. The majority's lot was glumly summed up by Adolphus Windeler, a German sailor turned prospector: "Hard times, hard work, & little gold."

Generally, the men who mined for pay fared better. Once a "hydraulic" mining company located paydirt, its high-pressure water hoses would collapse whole cliffs and direct the debris into long sluice runs that processed tons of material each day. The Malakoff mine at North Bloomfield sifted $4 million in gold out of 41 million cubic yards of earth in 22 years; and if its hired hands never got rich, at least they ate regularly.

Mining the newfangled hydraulic way, pipemen at the mile-long Malakoff pit aim high-pressure hoses to blast loose gold-bearing dirt and gravel. The jets of water, directed from nozzles known as Little Giants, were powerful enough to kill a man at a range of 200 feet.

Panning for gold in the 1850s, a group of freelance prospectors sifts through silt on a Sierra riverbank. Such groups often bought food and supplies in common and split the cost. But many a miner down on his luck had to pay his share by doing odd jobs or working part time for a local mining company.

Whitney's Band of Bold Surveyors

In 1860, the California legislature set up an agency to survey the state and collect samples of all its resources. Scientific knowledge was only part of the legislators' purpose; they also hoped that the survey would find gold. Headed by a cantankerous geologist named Josiah Whitney, the venture ran out of funds before completing its task. But Whitney's group did map the high Sierra, until then largely unknown.

Most of the Sierra exploration was done by six enthusiastic experts who started their work in 1863. Their first field leader was William Brewer, a shrewd, courageous botanist. The most colorful surveyor was Clarence King, who published melodramatic accounts of his exploits: " 'We're in for it now, King,' remarked my companion . . . but our blood was up, and danger added only an exhilarating thrill. . . .'' However, King suppressed such frills in his official reports. Describing the truly dangerous ascent of 14,018-foot-high Mount Tyndall, he wrote, "The summit was reached, without serious difficulty, after some risky climbing.''

Charles Hoffmann, a German-born engineer who acted as field chief of the survey in 1867, sets up his transit near the summit of the Sierra mountain named after him. His maps of the range established a cartographic standard that long outlasted the survey itself.

When the California Geological Survey began its official exploration of the Sierra in 1863, its members were, from left, Chester Averell, William More Gabb, William Ashburner, director Josiah D. Whitney, Charles F. Hoffmann, Clarence King and William H. Brewer. In 14 years of existence, the survey was often left short of funds by the state; the last of its many publications, a Yosemite guidebook, was printed at Whitney's own expense.

Dowd's Grove of Tall Timber

In 1852 a hunter named A. T. Dowd came upon a grove of trees so huge that his report of what he had seen was laughed off as a tall tale. Days later Dowd lured a few miners up to the grove, and crowed, "Now, boys, do you believe my big tree story?"

Dowd's report attracted widespread attention to the Sierra's sequoias, now known to be the largest living plants on earth. Though commercial logging operations did not begin in earnest until the 1860s, the wondrous size of Dowd's trees immediately attracted eager promoters whom John Muir called "laborious vandals." One stripped the bark off a live sequoia and displayed it in New York as "The Tree Mastodon: a mountain of wood." Another shill built a two-lane bowling alley atop a recumbent giant. The stump of a third sequoia was put to several uses. Smoothed off and roofed over, it served as a ballroom (for up to 48 dancers) and later as a stage for theatrical performances. Then in 1858, it housed the press and staff of a short-lived newspaper, *The Big Tree Bulletin and Murphys Advertiser.*

Loggers celebrate the felling of a giant sequoia with a solemn picture-taking ceremony. This tree, 26 feet in diameter at the base, yielded some 370,000 board feet of lumber—roughly enough to crate the liner Queen Elizabeth II.

Above Yosemite, two open-sided stagecoaches climb the switchbacks of Big Oak Flat Road, bound for Stockton. By 1903, when the picture was taken, the first automobiles were visiting the valley—and panicking the local livestock. The result: Cars were banned from Yosemite Valley until 1913.

Early Days in Hutchings' Eden

Rumors of lofty cliffs and waterfalls lured the first real tourist to Yosemite Valley in 1855. He was James M. Hutchings, an English-born journalist, and his florid travel articles about the valley attracted other sightseers. In Yosemite, Hutchings found both a passion and a profitable career. To accommodate the visitors, he bought and improved the Upper Hotel in the 1860s.

The future of tourism was assured in 1874, when two routes to the gold fields, the Big Oak Flat Road and the Coulterville Road, were extended on into the valley, permitting visitors to come by stagecoach.

When the coaches arrived, Hutchings' teen-aged daughter Florence, a reckless tomboy nicknamed Squirrel, acted as unofficial greeter. She would gallop out to meet the stagecoaches and race them back to the hotel. This performance scandalized some guests almost as much as the sight of Florence smoking a pipe.

Visitors to the valley in 1900 enjoy a pastoral jaunt against the backdrop of Yosemite Falls. A half century of tourism had raised the annual influx of sightseers to 10,000 and removed the earlier risks and discomforts of travel into the Sierra. The first visitors, proud of their daring and their purple prose, had braved bad roads and bad men to describe waterfalls as "living light from heaven" and themselves as "fearless spirits and noble hearted fellows."

Pausing in a sequoia grove, members of John Muir's Sierra Club enjoy an elaborate picnic during their annual outing in 1903.

2/ A Country Standing on End

*The signature of the glaciers is almost everywhere in the
Sierra—on almost every lake shore, every
headwall, every pass—for those who have eyes to see.*
WILLIAM O. DOUGLAS/ *MY WILDERNESS*

Not many years ago, a Sequoia National Park ranger strolled into the middle of a crowd of some 300 adventurous souls who had made a Labor Day climb from the Owens Valley to the flattish granite table that marks the summit of Mount Whitney. One hiker, awed by the sight of the two-mile plunge down to the valley floor, asked the ranger if he knew how the Sierra came to be shaped as it is.

"Well," said the ranger, who had a smattering of geology, "this summit plateau is part of the old landscape that was lying here as kind of a rolling lowland millions of years ago. Then the whole Sierra was bowed up like an arch." As he talked, other people turned to listen. "And then the keystone collapsed to form this great escarpment going down into the Owens Valley, with the White Mountains over there to the east making the other half of the broken arch. And later, through erosion and glaciation we got the final shaping of the land—the meadows and canyons and peaks and bowls—as you see them all around you today."

The ranger had paused to let that sink in, when a voice came from the crowd: "I don't believe anything you say. The Bible said the Lord made the world in six days, so nothing you say is true."

"Well, yes it does; it says that," replied the ranger, thoughtfully, and wandered off by himself to ponder the ultimate nature of geologic truth. Months later he had still not thought of a more suitable reply. "What could I tell the guy?" he shrugged. "Besides, maybe he was right."

Maybe he was. Today the most sophisticated earth scientists, not to mention the fundamentalists, are still groping among the particulars of the Sierra's creation. Some of those particulars (e.g., the role of sea-floor spreading in the Sierra's growth, the migration of silicon ions in the chemical weathering of certain granites) are stupefyingly abstruse. The wilderness traveler should think no more about them. But the main part of the Sierra story is as bold and dramatic as the mountains themselves. The evidence of mountain building and sculpturing is sticking right up where anyone can see it and shows in such a way that even the least-informed visitor can scarcely help becoming involved. It is all but impossible to look at Half Dome in Yosemite *(page 65)* and not wonder how it got that way: a 4,800-foot mass of granite whose face is a perpendicular wall and whose evenly rounded back would make a perfect mold for a massive concert shell. His first glimpse of the 10,895-foot wall of the Mount Whitney scarp so stirred Albrecht Penck, doyen of European geologists in the World War I era, that he asked to be left alone for some time that he might contemplate it in silence. Nor is it necessary to go to the Sierra's showplaces, since the landscape along almost any trail in the high wilderness is a beautifully disordered tableau of the Sierra's past, and all of it a part of the living present.

Near the waist of the Sierra, for example, there is a narrow path that climbs to a glacial bowl beneath the pinnacles of the Silver Divide. No guided tours go there. In fact, hardly anyone goes there at all, for the bowl lies several rough miles from any main trail, and the summit country around it has the angry look of land abandoned by growing things. The bowl holds no living glacier now, just snow remnants that endure through late summer, and in the bottom a deep green lake called Anne. I rode there one afternoon from a meadow campground farther down to get as far away as possible from every sign of people. The higher I rode, the closer I felt to the womb of the Sierra and the more intrigued I became by the circumstances of the mountains' birth and growth.

All mountain ranges are the result of the succession or interplay of fundamental forces within the earth. Some mountains grow primarily out of a single phenomenon, such as the protracted eruption of volcanoes. Others are the result of pressures that expand or contract the earth's crust in such a way that massive wrinkles called folds appear, or huge chunks break apart and move past each other along fracture lines called faults. The basic materials from which the bedrock of the mountains originally came may be sediments from ancient sea bottoms, or vast accumulations of fossilized marine organisms. They may be the

outpourings of volcanoes, or they may be molten bulges of rock called intrusions, which well up in partly liquid masses but stop and harden before breaking through the crust. At any time in its creation a mountain range may be eroded by streams, carved into bowls and U-shaped valleys by glaciers, honed into exotic shapes by wind, or quarried into pinnacles and blocks by the freezing and thawing of water. The Sierra is a living stage for virtually all these phenomena, which interacted in the past to create the range as it is today—and which are still contending to make the mountains into whatever they will be during some geologic tomorrow.

The lower trail to center stage at Anne Lake led out of a pine wood onto fields of smooth gray-white granite. Scattered about in the open were truck-sized boulders of a beige tinge, a different type of granite

from the bedrock they were sitting on. They had been carried here by a mountain glacier from their gestation ground miles away, and abandoned when the last of the deep ice melted off about 9,000 years ago. The proper name for them is "erratics," a word I can never remember; it keeps filtering imperfectly into my memory as "mavericks" or "nonconformists"—which is what these rocks really look like, sitting there in their mood of monstrous disarray.

Farther up, a cliff crowding close to the trail was split into vertical slabs by the freezing and thawing of water. One fracture, at least eight feet wide, ran through the granite for 200 feet, with rock fragments strewed along the steep floor of the cleft in a kind of staircase. Near the top of the stair, preserved by shade, was a wind- and water-sculpted monument of snow about 12 feet high, standing alone, touching no

Towering over Owens Valley, the eastern flank of the Sierra Nevada forms a wall 55 miles long and rises as high as 14,494 feet. This awesome escarpment, created partly by the uplift of the Sierra block, partly by the down-dropping of Owens Valley, gives dramatic evidence that it is still increasing in height: an uplift of a few feet occurred as late as 1872 when an earthquake devastated the valley.

walls. These fractures or joints invade most of the exposed granite of the Sierra, many of them running both vertically and horizontally in a single rock face. In some places the joints are so evenly spaced and close together they create symmetrical blocks that tumble out in time, eventually giving the mountainside the look of a man-worked quarry.

A quarter of a mile below the lake the trail petered out onto a sloping field of rock, and I dismounted to walk the last piece over rounded slabs made slippery by brown lichen. High above the lake, whose surface was being scratched on this blustery day by gray cats' paws, the torn skyline of the divide was almost entirely of light-gray granite; but in two places, hanging from the crest like dark tapestries, were remnants of the ancient stone that comprised this land before there was a Sierra. And in the rock by the lake's eastern shore was a concise, almost diagrammatic record of the turmoil in the bowels of the earth when the Sierra was being born. The face of one slab was inscribed with a narrow three-layered ribbon of stone—black-white-black—that had been contorted eons ago into four identical waves as steeply concave as those of a Japanese ink drawing of a storm at sea. In the trough of the fourth wave the ribbon broke off abruptly; then, offset some 14 inches, it started again to meander in curves and whorls along the rock —a perfect miniature of the folding and faulting that helped to shape these great mountains.

Oddly, this same slab was strewed with small bits of pumice, a porous volcanic stone so light that a piece tossed in Anne Lake floated for some time, until the water seeped into its microscopic pores. The pumice must have come here on the wind, for the nearest possible source was a pair of dormant craters, called the Red Cones, 10 miles away. The stones must have blown from there perhaps a thousand years ago, when superheated gases and molten matter burst through the twin fissures in a shower of red-hot rock and ashes. Such eruptions—often on a far more terrible scale—have tormented the Sierra for 150 million years, and there is no present sign that they will stop. In fact the lowlands beyond the Red Cones have an unfinished look, as though the earth is still wondering what to do. Hummocks and ridges of hardened lava poke up among the gray sweeps of desert sage. And in the meadows, dark clusters of pocked stone lie carelessly tossed about from recent outbursts whose residue of heat still issues from fumaroles and warm springs in the hills nearby.

There were other vivid signs of earth building in the sweep of the high valley dropping down from Anne Lake. Below the granite slope a

second, much larger lake, Peter Pande, had begun to silt in at the far end, eventually to become a meadow. It is in the nature of such ponds to fill slowly with the detritus of their feeder streams; and one day, where a half-mile stretch of water now glittered, there would be, instead, grass and a few lodgepole pines. Beyond Peter Pande the land plunged into the deep glacial trough of Cascade Valley, whose far wall was embroidered with cataracts formed when the ice mass pushed through the main valley and left the side streams hanging a thousand feet or more in the air. And among the heights still farther off was one of the most dramatic illustrations in the whole Sierra of the forces that created this wild country. Three long rockslides, each touching its neighbor, had spilled from the head of one minor peak whose rock strata were canted at an angle of some 60 degrees. The more distant slide was the deep red brown of rock that had been metamorphosed by subterranean heat and pressure, then oxidized when its surface minerals were exposed by erosion; the center slide was bright white, the freshly broken stone from a granite face; and the nearest slide was the blue black of old volcanic rock. Reining the horses close by these rockslides two days before the Anne Lake trip, a riding companion had said: "See how that granite pushed its way right up there between the volcanic and metamorphic rock? The rock is standing right on end. In fact, this whole country is standing on end."

This whole country—or at least large portions of it—has been standing on end for about 180 to 200 million years, since the fetal mountains first began to emerge from beneath the surface of a Paleozoic sea. Earlier the Sierra region had been under the ocean for the better part of 300 million years and perhaps longer. During that time, silt from coastal streams and the fine fallout from countless volcanoes settled in layers several miles deep upon the ocean floor. Then powerful contortions of the earth's crust folded and pressed in upon the compacted silt layers with enough force to change their chemical makeup so that one day they would show their faces in the high Sierra as the red brown of metamorphic rock or blue-black mutations of old volcanic waste. While the rocks hardened into permanent folds—macrocosms of the stone waves on the rock by Anne Lake—other forces within the earth broke the strata and crushed the enormous pieces together, sliding some beneath others until very slowly they reared against one another, finally to come to rest at violent angles.

During the later agonies of folding and faulting, masses of molten

The Evolution of Yosemite Valley

No one knows just how Yosemite Valley looked during the successive periods of its development over tens of millions of years. The paintings at right, commissioned to accompany a classic 1930 study of the region by François Matthes, are reconstructions of Yosemite's evolution as imagined by two artists who worked closely with the geologist.

The valley as we know it began to evolve when the streams and glaciers that carved it were established, about 500 million years ago. The reconstruction shown here begins after most of the initial Sierra uplift had been worn away by weathering and stream erosion.

1/ In what Matthes calls the broad valley stage, about 50 million years ago, Yosemite forms a wide trough framed by rolling hills less than 1,000 feet high. Through it meanders the Merced River, joined here and there by similar slow-flowing tributaries. Hardwood forests clothe the slopes. The climate is mild and rainy.

2/ The mountain valley stage, seen about 10 million years ago, marks a new period, when the crest of the Sierra began to rise as the whole range tilted westward. In the painting the Merced River, its course accelerated by this tilting, has cut the valley some 800 feet deeper than it had been during its broad valley stage. The climate has become cooler and drier, and as a result the hardwood forests have largely given way to conifers, among them sequoias.

3/ In the canyon stage about three million years ago, Yosemite, raised by the greatest Sierra uplift, has almost attained its present-day height. The Merced, transformed by the uplift into a racing torrent, has carved the valley into a canyon about 3,000 feet deep. The approach of the ice age has brought colder winters; the forests are thinning out.

4/ In the major period of glaciation 250,000 to 700,000 years ago, a blanket of ice, striped with dark moraines of rock rubble, almost fills the valley. The summit of Half Dome (top center) pokes up 700 feet above the glacier. But except for the tops of El Capitan and Eagle Peak, ice overrides all the highlands to the north (left).

5/ The ice sheet advances down the valley again. About 25,000 years ago, the Yosemite glacier, a smaller version of the earlier one, has extended only a short distance beyond Bridalveil Fall (bottom right). It has plowed through the valley, quarrying and polishing its walls and sharp cliffs. The climate is more moderate than during the earlier glaciation. Vegetation spreads in the valley beyond the glacier and atop the cliffs.

6/ At the beginning of post-glacial times, about 10,000 years ago, the glacier has melted away, leaving a high terminal moraine that dams up the valley below Bridalveil Fall, creating a broad lake about 800 feet deep. The Merced River is gradually filling in the lake with gravel, sand and silt, thus forming the level floor that Yosemite Valley displays today.

1/ BROAD VALLEY.

4/ MAJOR GLACIATION

2/ MOUNTAIN VALLEY

3/ CANYON

5/ LAST GLACIER

6/ EARLY POST-GLACIAL TIME

granite from far below started to force their way toward the surface, shouldering aside the existing stone. Where the overlying crust was weakest, some of the molten rock burst through to build volcanoes. But most of it stopped short of the ground level; there it cooled and hardened in the shape of great granite bubbles, the bedrock of the present Sierra Nevada. About 80 million years ago these granitic intrusions coalesced at the base into an almost solid underground flooring. Meanwhile the whole mass was slowly rising up, with the folded and broken layers of stone from the submarine time now lying atop the bedrock of granite. Streams formed and began to cut down through these overlying hills, wearing down the landscape from above as rapidly as it was rising from beneath.

In the southern and eastern Sierra, the streams and the rain that spawned them ate away the old rock cover until the domes and ridges of granite emerged to dominate the land, and there was little left of the ocean-laid metamorphic stone but isolated massifs like the Kaweah Peaks and the Minarets, or smaller remnants such as the darker rock-slides above Cascade Valley. To the north of what is now Yosemite some of these waterways cut through veins of quartz containing grains and masses of a bright yellow metal whose eroded pieces mingled as pebbles and dust among the stream-bed gravels. Then, between 30 and five million years ago, a sequence of volcanic eruptions buried the northern streams and valleys and all but the tallest peaks under thousands of feet of steaming mud.

Toward the end of this period the entire Sierra began to bow up strongly in a west-east arch—at least according to some geologists and to that earnest ranger on Mount Whitney. Moist winds rolled up the steepening slopes from the Pacific to drop snow and rain onto the highlands, creating new rivers and rich forest cover on the western flank, but leaving a rain shadow of parched land to the east. Like so many vestiges of youth, this weather pattern and other traits from Sierra's epoch of growth remained etched upon the character of the mountains.

Today the land to the east of the Sierra crest is still a desert, while blizzards continue to howl up the western slope, leaving some of the deepest snow anywhere in North America. During one stretch in 1969 it snowed for 30 days straight, forcing the Mammoth Mountain ski area in the east-central Sierra to close because the snow had buried many of the chair lifts; and in 1906-1907 a record of 73½ feet fell at Tamarack in the central Sierra. The melt from this annual snow cover still supplies the ground water for the superb trees of the western-slope forests. The

newer rivers born of the great snowpack have long since chewed down and back into the mountains. In the cutting, some of those rivers laid bare the yellow-spreckled gravels that had been buried under volcanic sludge; and in so doing they condemned all of California to quickened transformation from wilderness to the most populous American state.

On January 24, 1848, a carpenter named James W. Marshall saw golden flecks in the shallows of the American River near a sawmill he had built for an eccentric entrepreneur, Captain John A. Sutter. Marshall sifted an ounce and a half of the yellow stuff from among the sand and pebbles, and rode 30 miles to hand the bright dust to Sutter for testing. It tested out too well for the taste of Sutter, already a rich man whose dream was to maintain a pastoral utopia that would produce fat profits from more genteel ventures such as farming, ranching, real estate and the fur and grain trade.

"At once, and during the night, the curse of the thing burst upon my mind," wrote Sutter. "I saw from the beginning how the end would be, and the next day I had a melancholy ride to the saw-mill." Within a dozen years the recorded population of California had jumped 25-fold from the sparse 15,000 at the time of discovery. Sutter's kingdom had been trampled and the land stolen from him, and even the high fast-nesses of the Sierra were being clawed by gold-hungry forty-niners and their successors, the lumbermen and railroad builders.

Yet these latter-day scratchings by man, infected though they might become, were as nothing compared to the overwhelming violence with which nature, having exposed the gold in the old riverbeds, had gone about the penultimate forming of the Sierra. Somewhere between 10 and three million years ago, the apex of the west-east arch rose above 14,000 feet, the present elevation of the Sierra crest. During this same time several enormous keystone blocks in the arch, the biggest at the sites of the Owens Valley and the Lake Tahoe Basin to the north, worked loose along fracture lines in the bedrock and began to fall in crescendos of sound and power. For most of 10 million years the blocks continued to drop, with some of the most severe ruptures coming with-in the last 700,000 years. The worst of all came precisely that long ago when enormous quantities of volcanic matter began to spill out of fis-sures around a high plateau east of the present site of Mammoth Mountain. So much welled out that there was nothing left beneath the plateau to support it, and the entire land mass collapsed inward for some 2,000 feet to form the elliptical basin of Long Valley.

There is no way to establish a true knowledge of the awful force of these wrenchings that helped create the Sierra. But there was an indication not long after the Civil War when an earthquake split the floor of Owens Valley in a display that was sheer terror to virtually everyone who lived through it, but which in the great sweep of the Sierra's creation was no more than a single chord in a masterwork. For several hours one night in late March of 1872 severe tremors rumbled through the hills and tore at the earth around the little valley towns, particularly a hamlet called Lone Pine at the foot of the Mount Whitney escarpment. A contemporary account in a local newspaper began with a marvelous alarm-cry of headlines: "HORRORS! APPALLING TIMES! EARTHQUAKES! AWFUL LOSS OF LIFE! 25 PERSONS KILLED! HOUSES PROSTRATED! LONE PINE! ITS TERRIBLE CONDITION! MOST HEART-RENDING SCENES!"

A 40-acre field sank seven feet, a small lake disappeared and for a brief time the Owens River ran upstream until its bed was dry, the stranded fish flopping on the bare mud. "In the darkness," according to a later account, "people watched cascades of rock roaring down the mountains in monstrous avalanches, throwing out such brilliant trails of sparks that they were assumed to be flows of lava."

Over in Yosemite, about 120 miles from the epicenter of the quake but very much within the scope of its convulsions, John Muir reveled in the primeval glory of it all, having rushed from his cabin at the first tremor to greet this "noble earthquake."

"The shocks were so violent and varied," he wrote, "and succeeded one another so closely, that I had to balance myself carefully in walking as if on the deck of a ship among waves. . . . Suddenly there came a tremendous roar. The Eagle Rock on the south wall, about half a mile up the Valley, gave way and I saw it falling in thousands of great boulders . . . pouring to the Valley floor in a free curve luminous from friction, making a terribly sublime spectacle—an arc of glowing, passionate fire, fifteen hundred feet span. . . . The sound was so tremendously deep and broad and earnest, the whole earth like a living creature seemed to have at last found a voice and to be calling to her sister planets. In trying to tell something of the size of this awful sound it seems to me that if all the thunder of all the storms I had ever heard were condensed into one roar it would not equal this rock-roar."

Besides the rockslides, the greatest scar on the face of the whole Sierra from all this fury and sound was one wistful little breastwork threading across three miles of the Owens Valley floor and rising perhaps 23 feet at its highest point. The Sierra scarp looming over Lone

Pine stands almost 500 times as high—a crude measure of the wrenchings that attended its creation.

By tiny fits and grumblings the escarpment is still growing as the crestline of the range climbs through millennial inches and the unstable valley floor quivers with the 20-odd earthquake tremors that send subliminal shock waves through the mountains each year. For the last 300,000 years, however, nothing more violent than a 50-foot slip has occurred. In that time an entirely different force has finished the work of mountain-making by chiseling the heights into spires, carving and polishing the cliffs and bowls, and gouging out some of the deepest valleys in all America. "In the development of these," wrote the indefatigable John Muir, "Nature chose for a tool not the earthquake . . . but tender snow-flowers noiselessly falling through unnumbered centuries."

This was Muir's flossy way of bringing the Sierra glaciers onstage. Most earth scientists of the time—and particularly the pompous Josiah Whitney, leader of the first geologic survey to explore the Sierra—believed that the latter-day earth shaping had been done by rain and wind and stream flow. Dr. Whitney was a very big man; the greatest mountain in the whole range had been named for him, and he was loudly sure of himself. Especially he was sure that Yosemite Valley had been created by a monstrous collapse of the earth floor, and then further modified by weather and water. As for the dirty little ice fields still clinging to the shady sides of so many peaks, "It is doubtful whether these residual masses of ice can with propriety be called glaciers; they have no geological significance as such."

Muir thought otherwise. And one day in 1871 he found his proof, while following the course of a rivulet in a basin above the valley. "Tracing the stream back to the last of its chain of lakelets," he reported, "I noticed a deposit of fine gray mud on the bottom. . . . It looked like the mud worn from a grindstone, and," he added, giving himself all the intuitive best of it, "I at once suspected its glacial origin."

Muir was looking at what is now called glacial rock flour—microscopic grindings of stone scoured off by moving ice. Scrambling over a mound of earth from whose bottom the stream was issuing, Muir "was delighted to see a small but well-characterized glacier swooping down from the gloomy precipices of Black Mountain." Then in best Muir style he recalled having shouted to the winds, "A living glacier!" That ceremony over, he set about studying the curving barriers of earthen debris called moraines that marked the ice river's farthest line of advance;

and the following year he returned to confirm that the frozen body was indeed a living glacier by setting markers at its edge and periodically measuring the movement of the ice.

From this discovery and from later studies, Muir and others sketched out a pattern of glaciation of Yosemite, in fact for the whole Sierra. Somewhere back in time, they said, the range had been covered by an icecap, part of the vast, frozen sea thought to have inundated much of North America during a single glacial era that Muir and his contemporaries called the Great Ice Age. From the Sierra portion of the ice one minor tongue perhaps 4,500 feet thick had ground and scoured its way down Yosemite Valley, rumbling over some of the peaks and grinding them into the shape of domes, tearing the face off one great eminence to create Half Dome, and leaving the valley's side streams to plunge down granite cliffs for thousands of feet in the most spectacular set of waterfalls anywhere in the world. Then the whole North American ice field was supposed to have melted back, leaving as its residue in the Sierra little snippets of living ice.

As modern geologists have since confirmed, Muir was right about the role of glaciers in refining the face of the Sierra. An ice river did indeed carve out Yosemite and turn the side streams into spectacular falls, just as other Sierra glaciers carved their own cascaded canyons. But at the time when Muir first published his ideas, sophisticated techniques of geologic proof were not available. There was only visual evidence upon which to build a kind of pragmatic logic. And what Muir regarded as proof was not nearly good enough for the likes of crusty old Josiah Whitney, who felt that when he had said, "No glaciers," well then, "no glaciers" is what everyone should jolly well believe. "A more absurd theory was never advanced than that by which it was sought to ascribe to glaciers the sawing out of these vertical walls and the rounding of the domes," he rumbled. "This theory, based on entire ignorance of the whole subject, may be dropped without wasting any more time upon it." Muir, furthermore, was "a mere sheepherder, an ignoramus." So much for the messiah of the Sierra wilderness.

Nor was this blast the only heroic misfire by Whitney in the geologic field. Besides writing off Muir and the glaciers, and creating Yosemite Valley by a phantom earthquake, he was the bombastic victim of one of the most delicious frauds in the history of earth science. In February 1866 a report reached Whitney that an ancient skull, antedating by millions of years any previous human remains found in the Sierra, had been brought up from a mineshaft in the gold town of Cherokee Flat, in

Calaveras County. By no coincidence whatever, Whitney had long insisted that most scientists had been wrong in their estimates of the comparatively recent arrival of man, contemporaneous with the mastodon, in these mountains. Now here was the evidence, which Whitney hastened to pass around. "We have the skull at the office," Whitney wrote to his brother. "It is a bona fide find of the greatest interest, all the particulars of which I shall work up with the greatest care." He thereupon worked them up, to the accompaniment of approving nods from the guardians of such bastions of knowledge as Harvard and the *American Journal of Science.*

What Whitney did not know was that the particulars had previously been worked up with care by a bunch of local characters in Cherokee Flat. They had lifted the skull from a display in a doctor's office, had stuffed it into the gravel of the mine, and had then solemnly passed on the news to Whitney of a great anthropological breakthrough. The only security leak in the conspiracy was a poem published at the time by no less than Bret Harte, whose imaginary interview with the so-called Calaveras Skull follows, in part:

> *"Speak, thou awful vestige of the Earth's creation,—*
> *Solitary fragment of remains organic!*
> *Tell the wondrous secret of thy past existence,—*
> > *Speak! thou oldest primate!"*
>
> *Even as I gazed, a thrill of the maxilla,*
> *And a lateral movement of the condyloid process,*
> *With post-pliocene sounds of healthy mastication,*
> > *Ground the teeth together.*
>
> *And, from that imperfect dental exhibition,*
> *Stained with expressed juices of the weed Nicotian,*
> *Came these hollow accents, blent with softer murmurs*
> > *Of expectoration;*
>
> *"Which my name is Bowers, and my crust was busted*
> *Falling down a shaft in Calaveras County,*
> *But I'd take it kindly if you'd send the pieces*
> > *Home to old Missouri!"*

Whitney, as usual, ignored this bit of artful revelation. And Calaveras Man lived on in many corners of the anthropological world until

a scientific stake was driven through its heart in the form of several paragraphs of exposé in a learned paper titled *Tertiary Gravels of the Sierra Nevada of California,* published in 1911.

For all Dr. Whitney's stubborn pomposity, however, he should be judged kindly. For in perspective he was not much more wrong than a great many other men with a geologic bent; he was only noisier. In fact, he was really not much more wrong than Muir, who had been totally incorrect in theorizing that there had been a single uninterrupted Great Ice Age. There was no such thing—certainly not in the Sierra, where generations of glaciers came and went at least six times beginning two to three million years ago. Furthermore, the present Sierra ice fields are not leftovers from prehistory but the younger remnants of a cold cycle called the Little Ice Age that occurred as recently as the 15th to the 19th Centuries.

With the exception of Half Dome, which indeed had its face plucked at by ice, the glacial times had little to do with shaping the domes. These were made eons before when the upwelling granite cooled in the form of great bubbles; and they have kept their shape in a very odd manner. Instead of cracking horizontally and vertically like most granite, these massive domes shed outer layers of stone like an onion whose skin dries and cracks off. And there is no way of knowing when the rock will have an impulse to shed: a few years ago a ranger riding the ledge trail into Yosemite's Illilouette basin was thrown hundreds of feet to his death when the shelf he was riding on was sloughed off by its mother rock.

Even when old Josiah is judged in the light of the most modern knowledge, he turns out to have been not much more wrong than the ranger atop Mount Whitney who described the mountain's flat summit as part of a particularly old piece of landscape; the summit may be no older than any other piece of ground in the region, but just a trifle less eroded. For that matter Whitney was hardly less in the dark than the very finest of present-day geologists, who do not yet know why the Sierra granite surged up from below or why the mountains are still growing. In fact California's earth scientists recently fell to doubting whether there had ever been a Sierra arch at all, with keystones that collapsed to form the eastern valley; or whether the whole range had not been built by some other force not yet fathomed.

But like an understanding of sea-floor spreading and silicon ions, such scholarly doubts, with their attendant proofs and counterproofs,

probe a great deal deeper into the Sierra's origins than any ordinary wilderness traveler really needs go. And though such an attitude is perhaps irresponsibly antiscientific, I must confess that as just one more such traveler, I am perfectly happy with a concept like the fallen arch. Though I know it is controversial, it can still help me to understand my Sierra better and thus to love these mountains even more by feeling I know something of both their parts and the sum of them. In the same way, Muir's theory of a single Great Ice Age, with all its simple logic, is also good enough for me.

I do not really need to know the exact date of manufacture of the dizzy cliff my horse is skirting; it is enough that the precipice was made by a glacier, and that the mountainside is shining so brightly from the enduring polish left by the ice's passage that the light seems to come from within the earth itself. And I do not really need to know which of six or seven glaciers left scratches on the granite so subtle that some of them cannot be seen with the eye, yet can be felt by the soft pads of fingertips drawn across the face of the rock; it is enough that on a warm day I can lean against that scratched rock and dream of the time when the ice was here, and woolly mammoths crossed the frozen river stalked by the saber-toothed tiger and the dire wolf. And I do not need to know the glacial dating of the great bowl in whose clear lake I am fishing; it is enough that the trout are there, and the bowl is so vast a hiker walking away from me gets smaller and smaller until he simply disappears, having reached the vanishing point of his own size in distance. All that is good enough for me.

The Sculptured Rock

From almost anywhere on the rim of Yosemite Valley, a visitor can see a dramatic tableau in what is one of the world's great displays of sculptured granite—the Sierra. The colossal formations that make up the valley's walls show an incredible variety of contrasting shapes and textures: slab-sided cliffs and slender pinnacles, rounded domes and broad slopes of shattered rock. Granting that erosion works selectively, the visitor still may wonder how such a very hard granitic rock could have taken on so many different features.

The answer is far from obvious —but a close-up look at several rock surfaces yields a clue: most granite is crosscut by a grid of deep fractures called joints (because they resemble the masonry joints in a stone building). It is not yet known what causes these joints or why they occur in long parallel sets. But common sense suggests that the spacing of the joints is an important key to Yosemite's varied sculpturing: when the joints are separated by a relatively narrow interval, they weaken the whole structure of a rock formation and make it more susceptible to wear and breakup than it would be if its joints were farther apart.

The grand demonstration of this theory came during the ice ages. Rivers of ice more than 4,500 feet thick bulldozed through Yosemite Valley. Where these masses of ice pressed past rock formations whose joints lay tens or hundreds of feet apart, the surface was ordinarily strong enough to resist the glacier's ripping action. But where the joints were only a few feet apart, the glacier tore out blocks of granite, row upon row. This process, continuing for thousands of years, gradually deepened and widened the rocky contours of the valley until it acquired its present U-shaped profile.

The strongest formations are the domes, whose massive and gently rounded surfaces were relatively unmarked by passing glaciers. It was long believed that the domes were solid, jointless structures; therefore the term monolith was commonly applied to them. However, recent research indicates that the domes do have joints, though these are usually locked away safely far beneath the surface. A spectacular exception is Yosemite's Half Dome. A small section of this dome was weakened by jointing that reached the surface; exposed to glaciation and weathering, it gave way, leaving behind the slab of Half Dome's valley-side face.

Yosemite's Half Dome, photographed from Glacier Point, attests to the strength of ancient granitic rock. The clifflike wall of Half Dome was slightly convex before the retreat of the last glacier gave it the present shape about 11,000 years ago—but scientists believe that the ice sheets removed only a small fraction of the whole formation.

The Cracking, Peeling Domes

Though the Sierra's largely glacier-proof domes are its most durable formations, they are chronically subject to a peculiar process of destruction. The rounded surface of a dome tends to crack and peel off in concentric layers like the leaves of an artichoke. This stripping, called exfoliation, is not the result of wind and water wearing the surface; it is caused by pressures within the dome —huge expansive stresses that are relieved only when the granite surface bursts like an overinflated balloon.

In most domes, the surface peels off in layers less than 10 feet thick, though a few formations—among them Yosemite's Royal Arches—display broken layers over 100 feet thick. Each layer that peels off reduces the size of the dome, but leaves it smoother and more resistant. The oldest domes, which have been casting off surface layers for at least 12 million years, have changed very little in appearance.

Monuments Marking the Glacier's Wake

The abrasive rubble picked up by glaciers was dumped as much as 60 miles away from its origin. Among these deposits are the boulders at left, strewed in ones and twos by a melting glacier. Such stray boulders—some as large as a one-family house—were called erratics by early observers. At a loss to explain why they differed from the surrounding rocks, one theorist suggested that they had been washed from afar by Noah's flood.

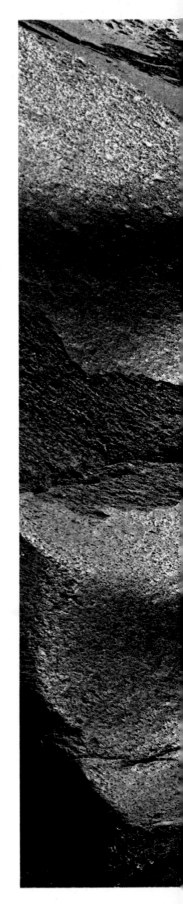

Seeded with abrasive sand and rock, glaciers ground broad tracts of solid Sierra granite to a high gloss. At right, a typical example of glacial polish gleams on a wall above Tuolumne Meadows in a canyon adjoining Yosemite Valley. The polish also glints through the waters of Tenaya Creek, which the Indians called Py-we-ack, "stream of the glistening rocks." A sheen on the rock signals a victory for granite in its clash with a glacier. While heavily jointed rock yielded to glacial pressure, sparsely fractured granite stood firm. Confronted by such obdurate stone, the mightiest glacier could do no more, over millennia, than shine up the stone's surface.

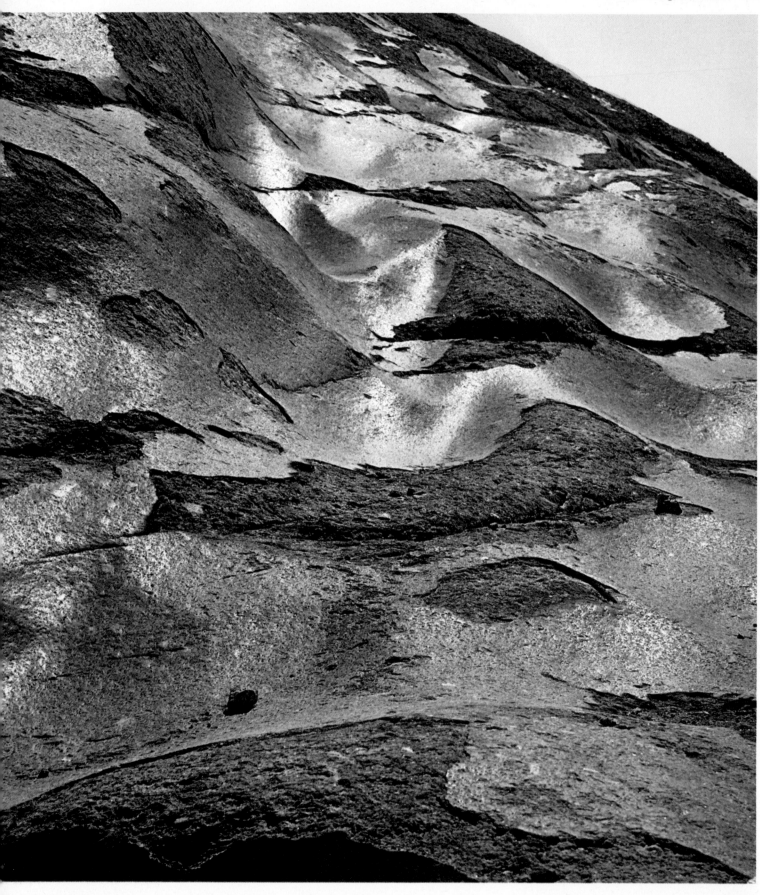

Terraces Carved by Ice and Rain

Ice-age glaciers did the major work of remodeling the Sierra by a ripping process called quarrying; it left behind spectacular sculptures like the terrace at left, whose sharply etched features indicate a relatively recent geological origin—only 10 times as long ago as the birth of Christ.

The glacier, inching downhill with its inner ice melting in the heat generated by the pressure of thousands of feet of compacted snow, pumped water into the granite's joints, which generally run in vertical and horizontal sets. Freezing—and expanding—inside the joint, this runoff gradually pried loose a section of rock. When the section was loose enough, the movement of the glacier carried it off. By removing millions of individual blocks and slabs, this process quarried granite hundreds of feet thick, creating not only the terraces but also great gulches and overhangs.

A terrace (right) exposed to the elements far longer than the one at left shows the softened outlines caused by the weathering of granite blocks and slabs left behind by the glaciers. Expanding ice pried open larger and larger clefts and exposed more and more surface to the weather. At the same time the rock surface was crumbling, bit by tiny bit, under the attack of rain and meltwater charged with acids from decaying vegetation. As the blocks and slabs were slowly rounded and softened by erosion, crumbled particles of rock gradually sifted down to the foot of the terrace and decomposed into soil.

3/ The Range of Light

The impression is one of grandeur, but at the same time of desolation — the dark pines, the light granite, the absence of all sounds except the sighing of the wind through the pines...
W. H. BREWER/ *UP AND DOWN CALIFORNIA IN 1860-1864*

It is noon. And my horse stands, belly heaving from the morning climb, at the crest of Duck Pass, gateway between the bustling settlement of Mammoth Lakes basin on the eastern slope and the 503,258-acre John Muir Wilderness. Never among any mountains, nor perhaps anywhere on earth, have I seen a richness of color to match the spectrum along this trail. The natural tones range from the white of tiny snow fields tucked into shaded gullies on peaks above the lake to the blue black of ancient volcanic outcroppings among the granite. At this moment Duck Lake just below me is most dramatic. It measures some 258 acres on the surface and 300 feet deep, and its color is the same perfect blue of the ocean that I have seen in Davis Strait between Baffin Island and Greenland, and in the Pacific where the trade winds roll down to Hawaii. Only very deep water takes on this hue, and the lake's bottom contours, scooped out by a glacier, are indeed so profound that the water soaks up every color in the spectrum but the blue.

Beyond the meadow the water vanishes in a drought-shriveled cascade; but from the look of the land below, the symphony of Sierra color will continue all day as our pathway drops through switchbacks and long undulations toward the valley campground by Fish Creek. Muir himself was so dazzled by the Sierra's brilliant tones, its mirror lakes and shining granite that he called these mountains the Range of Light. There is another name, an Indian word, that I like better: Inyo,

the Dwelling Place of a Great Spirit. The Paiutes, who roamed the eastern foothills and valleys until the white man came, first gave the word to the mountains east of Owens Valley, and now this section up to the crest of the Sierra bears it as well, as part of the Inyo National Forest. Here dwells Numunana, the People Father, with whom the Paiutes spoke as they traveled the wilderness. They spoke, too, with the guardian powers that are within all the rocks, the snow, the trees and wild things. They drew strength from these powers, and from the wind, too, and from the blue desert haze that often hangs over the valley.

No part of the Sierra belongs to the Paiutes now; but the rightful name for this land of austere beauty will always be Inyo, for the high country remains the dwelling place of a great spirit. Among these granite crests there is an aura of exhilaration, of awe and fulfillment. To one who knows the Sierra well and comes back to the high country after having been away for a time, there is, too, the joyous rush of recognition that strikes a sailor walking the streets of a city when a sudden turn of wind brings him the sea air. Seeing Inyo now bathed in the clearest light of noon, I feel once more the wish that no one had ever been in this Wilderness before. At least, no white man.

Yet along the approaches to the wild country the presence of 20th Century white man has been pervasive. On the way up this morning we passed dozens of people, some of them hunkered down beside lakes and streams to fish or snooze, others sifting along the trail with us. Among the walkers was a scattering of pale-skinned city couples, the men with notably smooth faces and combed hair, the women in slacks and cardigan sweaters thrown over T-shirts. They have headed back to the parking lots at the Mammoth Lakes roadhead, having taken their little nibble of the Sierra. And although this is their land as much as ours, it is hard not to feel intruded upon by them.

There has also been a sense of intrusion from the obvious management of the trail itself. Rangers from the U.S. Forest Service, which administers this sector of the Sierra, have carried aside all loose stones. At short intervals small logs called water bars have been embedded slantwise in the path to lead off snowmelt and rain so the trail does not erode as a sluiceway. At longer intervals but with insistent frequency, small wooden signs tell the traveler exactly where he is (Duck Lake Trail, Reds Meadow 9 miles; John Muir Trail 5 miles; Purple Lake 8 miles), with arrows pointing down the various branch trails.

About an hour back we passed an even bigger sign announcing the border of the Muir Wilderness: WELCOME TO THE BACK COUNTRY, ENJOY IT,

PRESERVE IT. Surely, we felt, from here on the human presence would be less noticeable.

Immediately we encountered more people. However they were a different sort, and to them, we were the intruders. Down from the last pitch to Duck Pass came two young men, strong, tanned, unshaven, one with his hair pulled back by a bandanna. They were backpackers, and from the look of them they had been out a week, their sunburned legs bared by old shorts and their feet laced into dusty hiker's boots. Forest Service rules require backpackers to give way on the trail to horses. Silently the two men half stepped, half stumbled into a small gully, a look of harsh impatience in their eyes. (Backpackers do not like horses, which chew up the trail with their iron shoes and leave their droppings everywhere—a pollution, says the hiker, of the natural environment.)

The two young men near Duck Pass said nothing at all as we rode by. And though they looked unhappy with us, we were relieved, in certain ways, to see them. Their shaggy, weathered appearance contrasted sharply with that of the people on the lower trails, promising wilder land ahead and suggesting a reassuring image of the wilderness as a target with concentric rings, each having its own character and denizens. The bull's-eye is the pure wild—such places as Anne Lake on the heights beyond Fish Creek, or Simpson Meadow in Kings Canyon, or the Lake Italy Basin, lying below the 13,000-foot heights of Mounts Hilgard and Abbot. Surrounding such bull's-eyes are lesser degrees of wildness, from the barest high trails and spartan bivouacs to the manicured paths lower down. The outer ring is the roadhead with its parking lots and managed campgrounds, its bungalows and rental rowboats, all reachable by auto-borne day trippers.

Now, as our horse party crests Duck Pass, we are moving into the second ring of the target, closer to the heart of Inyo. And we notice that on this day the spirit of the mountain seems unsettled, for he is speaking in a tone very different from summer's gentle whispers. Today the spirit is letting us know it is his pleasure to change the season, to change the look of the land. And his warning shout comes rushing heavily through the constriction of the pass, tearing at the stunted mattings of whitebark pine that are the only vestiges of trees to survive here at timber line. The air has a touch of dampness to it, and the wind has bent the wisps of clouds capping the tallest crags into convex curves; their shape is a sign of the celebrated Sierra wave, the high-rising air current that glider pilots the world over come to ride—and announces, too, a deep mutation in the mountain weather.

We have chosen to ignore the warning voice, moving on into the back country, though each of us knows that winter is poised to sweep down from the north, and tonight's dry campground may by morning be a whitened mess of wet saddles, buried food stores and ice-stiffened cinch ropes. The plants and wild creatures of the mountain have heard the voice, too, but they are heeding its message in ways that their genes have dictated over unending centuries. In damp gullies below us the catkins of the willow shrubs have gone to fruit, their seeds tufted with feathery white fibers to carry them on the wind to fresh ground where they will germinate after the snow has come and gone. Along the draws much lower down the aspen leaves are purest gold from the nightly frosts that have ended the growing season's production of green chlorophyll, so the leaves show only their residual yellow pigments before they drop to the ground. At trail's edge, mint-smelling pennyroyal blossoms have turned to brown crumbles as the plant dies back to its roots to conserve energy for next year's short growth burst.

A tiny alpine chipmunk has left a neat pile of pine-cone husks on a rock where he has been separating out the seeds to bury in pugholes —tiny storage pits—spotted around his terrain. But he will never eat them, for at our horses' approach he skitters over a rise in the open ground and a Cooper hawk, which has been cruising on the buffeting wind, starts down at him in scalloped swoops. The denouement is not visible, but I would be reluctant to bet on the chipmunk.

A wiser creature, the pika, keeps hidden inside the entrance to his rocky den, showing no part of himself but making a nasal complaint at our interruption of his last days of preparation for winter. A fist-sized ball of fat and gray-brown fur, the pika is vaguely related to the rabbit. During the warm weeks just ending, he has gathered bits of grass and plant stems and set them to cure in tiny piles like hay in the sun before storing them as winter forage. Today he is nearly ready to call it a season and go to ground under sheltered ledges in the debris of a rockslide, where he will spend the snow time nibbling on the cubic yard of hay he has hidden there.

Unlike the horse party clattering across his habitat, the pika came to the Sierra crest with the basic design for high-country living. It is really an arctic species that migrated here with the glaciers and was marooned on these cold islands of high altitude when the ice receded. Some of the plants, too, have arctic origins that imbued them with the ability to survive in timber line's bitter climate. The green and white

splash of saxifrage beneath a rock overhang as we start down toward the lake is identical to a saxifrage that grows at sea level on Devon Island inside the Arctic Circle.

But to the saxifrage, life in the high Sierra is not very good, and in some ways the plant might have been better off if it had stayed home on Devon Island. There it would have just as long a growing season as the 40-odd days it will likely have to settle for here next summer, if the coming winter is as long and hard as the wind's voice promises. And there it would not have to endure mid-July snow flurries or the 80° heat of a Sierra summer afternoon. Still the saxifrage has managed to make an accommodation to the Sierra's demanding range of temperature by putting down its roots in damp, shaded places where the August heat cannot kill it. And it has made an accommodation with the short growing season by staying small: the stem measures only two to four inches, a growth the plant can achieve during the brief weeks of warmth in this spartan seedbed.

Though such accommodations are so logical as to seem almost cozy, none of these vegetal dwarfs really has a pleasant time of it. "Up here in these higher altitudes," explains one of my riding companions, a lady whose devotion has been the ecology of the high Sierra, "you're looking not at the plants and trees that are happy here, but the ones that are less unhappy." By this theory of environmental negativism none of the hunched and often homely alpine growths is at home in the lonely reaches of timber line and above; yet by reluctant necessity they have worked out their marginal modus vivendi in surroundings that would kill off any lush lowland species.

A tree like the whitebark pine grows as a sort of creeper vine along the ground instead of reaching upward into the shrieking wind. Its tough, supple branches are so closely matted that they offer a snug shelter for any hiker or coyote or bighorn sheep that is wise enough to crawl down into them during a mountain storm. During the short summer the tree may restrict its growth to no more than an eighth of an inch, and a limb the thickness of a soda straw can be as much as 75 years old. Thus the whitebark, less unhappy at altitude, lives. Yet if a whitebark attempts to move down the slope, it cannot compete with the bigger, handsomer conifers that themselves are unable to survive in the harsh world farther up.

When our horses reach the final switchbacks down to Duck Lake, the whitebark in fact concedes the ground to lodgepole pines scattered in open stands and to spires of blue-green hemlock. The dwarf flowers,

too, give way to the taller yarrow and wild onion, each one browned by fall, and to heather and Indian paintbrush whose seasonal red has managed to survive the frost. Down at the lake a meadow bordering the outlet stream shows signs of still another change in the look of things. Every grassy corner and every grove of trees contain a rubble of fire-scarred rocks left by weekend campers who habitually stay here for the night, having reached the limit of a comfortable one-day hike from the roadhead back at Mammoth Lakes. "People tend to bunch up at imaginary boundary points like that," a ranger had told us in some disgust, "and it makes a mess." It surely does, and the U.S. Forest Service has not yet been able to prevent it.

Where the meadow meets the lake, a weir of rock with the weathered wooden slats of a fish barrier in the middle stretches across the mouth of the outlet stream. It was put there by the California Department of Fish and Game, custodian of the creatures in this wilderness (animals and fish in most national forests are managed by state agencies). The barrier's purpose was to maintain a balance of fish life the department itself had created in waters that had been barren. In ages past there had been no rainbow trout here or in most of the other 2,000 lakes and ponds in the Sierra. The glaciers scoured out virtually all aquatic life from the high lakes and later dug through the valleys to chop off the outlet streams from those lakes to form cascades. Native rainbow in the waters at lower altitude were unable to battle their way up the waterfalls to the high lakes—but they did remain in such valley waters as Fish Creek. There, as the name implies, they still thrive.

Beginning about 1870 various anglers, and later the Fish and Game people, sprinkled rainbow and brook trout around the high lakes. They also transplanted some golden trout from the southern Sierra. And they built barriers and weirs to keep everything in its new habitat. Whereupon the fish, in the manner of most wild things, began to behave in all sorts of spontaneous and undignified ways that no one had anticipated.

At Duck Lake some of the goldens mated with their close cousins, the rainbows, to spawn a race of mongrels; and the rest of the goldens fell victim to the cannibalistic tendencies of the highly prolific brook trout, a species that tends to eat its neighbors rather than marry them. Once the fish had finished mating or murdering, however, few of them really prospered. For a lake in the high Sierra, like the land itself, does not provide enough nourishment to support a strong food chain. There are too few algae to feed many crustaceans and other crawly things,

which are thus too sparse to fatten up the trout. But in the years following World War II the Department of Fish and Game planted trout in virtually every food-poor high Sierra puddle big enough to hit with an airdrop of hatchery fingerlings. Naturally most of the trout stayed hungry. "Some of these mountain fish are so starved they grab at anything that even looks like food," says the other lady in the party, a Montana ranchwife with a saddlebag full of trout flies and spinning gear. The trout also tend to stay small. A pond not far from Duck Lake once yielded up a 20-year-old brook trout measuring almost eight inches and weighing perhaps a quarter of a pound (with decent food a brook trout can grow a pound a year).

In a recent burst of experimentation designed to provide bigger fish rather than just busy fishing, the department introduced into Duck Lake the Kamloops, a salmonlike strain of rainbow native to British Columbia. The Kamloops have got on handsomely, growing up to three pounds on a diet of available crustaceans supplemented by the Sierra's terrestrial insect life, which prospers in the wet shore grass through spring and summer but which, mercifully for our particular party, expires with the coming of heavy frost.

The sum total of the Department of Fish and Game's busy hand, the planted species and the weirs and barriers, is unquestionably good fishing. In the broader sense it might be called good recreational planning for the increasingly heavy numbers of people who come into the Sierra. I would call it nothing of the kind, for it raises a disturbing question: should there be all this fiddling in a wild preserve that Congress has said must retain "its primeval character . . . with the imprint of man's work substantially unnoticeable"?

At least one of my mountain companions thinks not. "Even some of our Fish and Game biologists are beginning to feel that the problems we've got up here are entirely man-caused," she says. "Our fish populations had reached equilibrium. But we kept putting our grubby fingers in there, overexploiting, letting one species take over from another. It's improper land use."

I agree with the lady. As I have told you before, this is *my* Sierra. I know just how the place should be run.

On the other hand our horse packer and guide, a devout angler, cannot believe anyone could be so stupid as to think as I do. He likes his lakes full of trout and is dead set against pulling out the weirs. "All the trout would swim over the falls," he says, "and we'd lose them." He speaks with the blunt conviction of a lifetime outdoorsman. He is, in

fact, a third-generation Californian whose great-grandfather ran firearms and supplies to the Sierra hideaway of two antiestablishment gunslingers in the 19th Century. The strain of hard-nosed independence is still strong in the family blood, and the packer is profanely certain the Sierra is his. No one else has the insight to manage it properly, particularly the Forest Service, which he feels has blundered with a new directive to dismantle permanent back-country fireplaces as inconsistent with a true wilderness philosophy. "Look at all them fire rings," he booms, sliding from his horse. "Why don't the Forest Service keep one permanent fireplace to concentrate the mess?"

With that he unhitches the lead ropes to let the horses and mules graze awhile, and plops down against a tree to begin stuffing his mouth with massive hunks of sandwich. The rest of us dismount to chew on our lunch and wash it down with lake water. Afterward I fold my jacket and hat against a boulder away from the wind, scooch my back in the sand and pine cones to make a smooth depression, and doze as the low chuckling of the stream and the soughing of the midday wind play a gentle duet around me.

I awaken to find the packer sitting next to me. And I ask him why, with all the water and grass and good brush cover along the trails, we have not seen a single deer since we came into the wilderness. He laughs and tells me I am in too much of a hurry. Whenever people come into the wilderness, he says, they are greedy for a quick look at the biggest and best of the wildlife. Yet almost half of all Sierra visitors never see anything bigger than a chipmunk. For wilderness is not a condensable experience wherein the creatures scurry by in an enchanting parade, performing cute little rituals as they might in a Disney fantasy. The larger animals, particularly the predators, make their living by staying out of sight as much as possible, both from simple native caution and from having been shot at for over a century.

The mountain coyote of the Sierra has been a career target for sheep ranchers, particularly in the foothills where stockmen fire away at any wild dog unwise enough to show his face. Therefore the coyote tries not to. The mountain lion, more lethal as a predator and therefore deeply disliked by stockmen, is of an even more private persuasion. The deer, too, are man-shy—that is to say, gun-shy—and it takes patience, luck and a practiced eye to see them with any regularity. In a recent survey a group of casual hunters reported spotting seven deer over two days in an area where a trained naturalist had counted 60. Since our

own counts thus far have been zero, the packer takes care to explain where the deer might be if any of us would learn how to pay attention.

"See that up there by the pass?" he asks, pointing to a little hanging meadow southwest of the notch we came over this morning. His finger indicates a faint zigzag thread of trail traced across the open ground. He explains that the trail was not made by people. Rather it is the main deer migration route out of the summer feeding ground in the valley of the Fish Creek region. Through these fall days the deer have stayed down in the moist, protected bottoms, fattening on aspen and willow and other tender shoots. When dustings of sleet and snow begin to blow in, they will become restless. Then with the first heavy blizzard they will start out over the pass and down Mammoth Creek to their winter range in the eastern lowlands. It is still too warm for them to begin moving, the packer says. Nevertheless, if we look sharp, tonight along the creek, or tomorrow morning in the meadows, we may see a few.

When we remount, the horses turn reflexively back toward the pass, having been heavily programed to do so by a lifetime of day rides out of the Mammoth stables. They are not at all pleased to be thumped and reined around until they are pointing the other way. They bridle at the signposted junction where the Duck Lake Trail runs into the Muir Trail, making it altogether clear that they may yet decide to go home for the night. During the ensuing 20 minutes or so, there is a shared and stubborn uncertainty between horse and rider about who is *numero uno*. Naturally I make every outward sign it will be me. But secretly, like any dude in his bright new Levi's, I am not at all convinced. Nor, for that matter, is my horse. We have been on the trail only one day, and I am very conscious of being too fresh from the city myself, too soft of hand and foot, and not a little uncertain of the land ahead.

In addition to these qualms of the spirit, a very real physical crisis has arisen from the conformation of the horse. Whereas the legs of a movie cowboy seem to drop comfortably down into his stirrups, the legs of an ordinary mortal are forced outward by the horse's rib cage and then pulled inward by the slant of the dangling irons. For a middle-aged rider this causes some exquisite agony in the knees. During the morning it has helped—though not much—to dismount periodically and walk along beside the horse, thus preventing obsolescent joints and ligaments from freezing altogether in the pain of unfamiliar positions. Gradually, however, like the whitebark on the mountain, horse and rider are reaching an accommodation.

Not a moment too soon. Suddenly, though the symphony of color

Seeming to grow from naked rock, a Sierra juniper clings to an exposed slope, its gaunt branches pulled to one side by the unrelenting force of the wind. Its plant neighbors growing on higher ridges are dwarfed and gnarled by steady 60-mile-an-hour gales.

82/ **The Range of Light**

still plays around us and the air has warmed to early afternoon, the character of the trip changes frighteningly. Up to this point we have been on wide, gradual trails, on lake shores and near beaten-down campgrounds. We have been safe, cruising rather than adventuring. Now, however, we are threading our way along the side of a chasm and have just crossed an avalanche gully bisecting the trail. The Sierra rock is everywhere—not just grandly in the distance but very much underfoot in loose stones and ahead in slick, slanted slabs the horses must negotiate. Around the next bend the land below the trail disappears altogether, and through a break in the treetops I can see just under my right boot a gorge so deep and steep-sided that the bottom is not yet visible, even here from the edge.

A little giddy from the altitude, I have slipped my boots away from the stirrups so as to be able to bail out quickly if the horse makes a significant misstep. This precaution turns out to be silly, since all the pack-train animals are beautifully steady and every bit as interested in survival as their riders. Nevertheless, the fear of heights is a powerful force, and like most lowlanders I will never conquer the habit of leaning slightly toward the mountain at such places, a practice that visibly irritates any horse since it pulls him off balance.

At this unhappy moment, with my psyche wrapped in a moist blanket of acrophobia, a pair of jet fighters from nearby Edwards Air Force Base blasts close overhead, splitting the air with their thunderous whistle. I shorten the reins and set my feet back into the stirrups to hold the horse from shying. But when the supersonic boom comes he does not even quiver. He has been through this mountain cleft so often, with the stunting pilots roaring in just beyond the treetops, that he no longer notices. Yet I cannot adjust as well as the horse. Mingled with plain fright is a surge of anger; the sound of the jets is terrible, the screaming voice of war, and it has no place in the wilderness. No place on earth, really, but surely no place here, where people come to be at peace with the earth and with themselves.

The trail takes a turn away from the canyon and onto a 50-degree sloped hillside spotted with timber. Just below us is the first juniper I have seen on this trail, a stunted, wonderfully ugly brute of a tree that seems totally unlike its slender garden-variety relative cultivated on New England lawns. The massive cinnamon-colored trunk of this Sierra juniper, like so many others near timber line, is perhaps four or five feet thick, with the top blasted off about 20 feet up by wind or lightning and the

branches streaming off to leeward from the prevailing westerlies. It looks, in all, like an unfinished window display whose top section and other branches never arrived for assembly. Yet there is about it an enduring quality, a homely strength that suggests many seasons and many lives will come and go before this juniper is done.

As if in confirmation, the juniper's bulk rises at the very edge of an avenue of smaller lodgepole pines whose own trunks are broken off eight or nine feet above the ground—the level at which winter avalanches have roared over the deep snowpack, destroying everything tall enough to poke above the surface. Among the tall stumps a rumpling of green shrubs has sprouted, as they typically do along avalanche tracks where the overshading trees have been destroyed and the soil stirred up to create a more hospitable seedbed.

The trail descends rapidly now, along the Purple Lake outlet and down toward Fish Creek in the ultimate valley. The soil all along the slope has had only the barest sprinklings of summer rain to bring life to it. This is typical of the eastern part of the Sierra, where the parched earth supports a more modest race of growing things than does the wetter western region. Certain pines, however, are fond of the crumbly, quick-draining mineral soil. In the higher reaches, the lodgepoles hog the best seedbeds by casting an inhibiting shade and by dropping tannin- and resin-bearing needles and cones that virtually prevent anything else from growing. "A high-altitude desert," the packer calls it. And indeed there the forest floor is bare of everything but a thin litter of cones and needles, looking almost as though it had been cleared and raked. But here below the 9,700-foot level, where the slopes begin to ease toward the valley, the earth holds its moisture better. In fact, the entire climate is measurably milder. The peaks shield the trees and plants from the tearing wind, and for each thousand feet of descent the temperature has risen about 3°, warming the middle-elevation flora so it can grow more profusely.

Although lodgepoles continue to poke up along the trail, the dominant tree is now the Jeffrey pine, a handsome giant of 100 feet and more whose coarse brown bark cracks with the tree's growth into four-sided plates like the skin of an alligator. The bark of one Jeffrey shows a yellow rip exposing a panel of sap-beaded wood, the wound measuring some two feet across and running 20 feet down the trunk to the ground. A bolt of lightning hit this tree two summers ago, apparently condemning it to a slow death that has already denuded its upper branches and turned the long silky needles a dry brown. The root but-

Patterns of Bark—
the Trees' Signatures

From a distance, the trees that forest the Sierra at middle altitude seem uniform: stand after stand of hardy cone-bearing evergreens. Although each species of coniferous tree, when seen close up, has its own definite characteristics (of size, color, shape of cones and needles), the most obvious clue to identity is the tree's protective sheath, its bark.

Bark is the product of the cambium tissues, the growing layer of a tree. The cells of these tissues are constantly dividing to create new cells; those on the inside of the layer form new wood while those on the outside become fresh bark.

This replenishing is needed not only to replace pieces that have sloughed off to accommodate new growth, but to restore bark seared by fire or gouged by animals.

The photographs on these two pages show barks of the seven common Sierra conifers. The trees are strikingly different in four ways:
□ Color, determined by the bark's chemical composition, ranges from the deep reds and purples of the giant sequoias to the silver of the Western white pine.
□ Thickness and density vary from the soft, bulky "plates" that cover the Western yellow pine to the thin, hard casing of the California red fir.
□ Texture may be deeply fissured, as on the Jeffrey pine; filigreed with irregular scales, as on the sugar pine; or relatively smooth, like the finely grained bark of the lodgepole pine.

SEQUOIA

YELLOW PINE (PONDEROSA)

JEFFREY PINE

WESTERN WHITE PINE

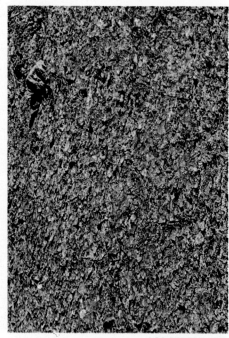

LODGEPOLE PINE

RED FIR

SUGAR PINE

tresses are charred, and vestiges of a ground fire reach out to a radius of about 30 feet, where the fire spent itself, having come to bare soil at the outer edge of the Jeffrey's needle fall.

Such minor lightning fires are common through the high Sierra in late summer and fall; in this very district they occur anywhere from 15 to 120 times in a single year. They are, in fact, as much a part of the natural ecology as the sun and rain. And in some areas at elevations above 8,000 feet the rangers no longer try to put them out, having finally embraced a bit of wisdom any Indian could have shared with them 100 years ago: regular small fires may be healthy for a woodland. They creep around eating up dead underbrush and other forest litter and clean the soil. They open the ground for new sprouts of underbrush the deer can feed on and for nut-bearing bushes to nourish the smaller animals. Some Sierra trees are actually stimulated by fire. The giant sequoias and Jeffreys can best seed themselves in ground that has been cleansed by fire. And one tree, the knobcone pine, cannot sprout at all until the heat of a fire cooks open the cones to let the seeds drop out.

Beyond the small burn the forest floor has a green quilting of chaparral, a mixture of various hard-limbed shrubs common to the Sierra and the adjacent California valleys. About half of it here is buckbrush, a gray-green bush with fragrant leaves and shoots that are a favorite browse for the deer herds. Peering into one thicket I have a wistful hope that any moment, if I look in just the right place, a doe may come slipping through with her hopping, stiff-legged gait. But not today.

The remainder of the undergrowth is manzanita, whose sweet berries and tangle of tough branches provide a safe and profitable foraging ground for rodents and small birds. Manzanita is Spanish for "little apple," after the ruddy-skinned apple-shaped beads of fruit that sprout among the bright green leaves. As we ride along, a scurry of chipmunks and ground squirrels is busy feeding on remnants of the fall-dried fruit, while black-headed juncos flutter among the branches looking for any berry that might not yet have fallen. "The junco," explains one of my companions, "is the most abundant of all our Sierra creatures. And," she adds with scientific solemnity, "the most successful therefore." Being basically nonscientific, I tend to equate success in wild animals not with numbers but with regal presence. And I am therefore much more impressed by a flight of five mountain quail that flashes up in a flutter of blue gray, the dark crest of one cock sweeping back proudly.

It is past 5 when we finally dismount at our campground in a grove

of pines and turn out the pack animals in hobbles for the night. The center of the camp is at a sharp bend in the winding course of Fish Creek. Upstream a flat meadow becomes a marshy catch basin for Fish Creek's overflow. Early one season the packer caught a trout by casting into a puddle right in the middle of fresh green grass. In fall, however, the sumps are gray-brown circles of parched mud, and the minor watercourses leading into the creek have become bright pathways of rounded pebbles. The grass is dry, and it looks invitingly soft in the late afternoon sun, a tempting place to lay a sleeping bag. But we will pitch our tents in the grove where the ground is a foot or two higher and free of the evening damp that rises from the meadow to chill a sleeper even in this dry season.

As we walk down to the stream to take up water for the evening meal, a rainbow trout flashes away, and we can see two or three brook trout holding under a log in one of the stills. The packer and I set up our fly rods and make a cursory pass at several pools. But it is quickly growing dark, and the fishing is a formal gesture on our part just to certify that we are now firmly entrenched in the wilderness.

The ladies have generated a fire beneath a pot of stew that, while unquestionably nourishing, has the specific gravity of a sash weight. Nevertheless it fills an enormous gap in the stomach. After dinner, while we are climbing into long underwear and ski parkas against the fast-coming night cold, a full moon rises, etching the treetops' silhouettes against the brilliant glow of granite ridges, and keeping the Sierra alive with color even into the night. We have heaped the fire with pine knots that burn with bright fragrance from their impregnations of pitch. My tent door faces the fire, whose reflections and shadows run in swift waves along the tent roof. They are the last things I see before dropping into a deep and perfect sleep to awaken to a clear morning, the fire crackling afresh beneath the coffeepot, and the horses and mules rolling in the meadow as the sun moves down the west wall of the valley to reach into our campground.

A Continent on a Mountain

PHOTOGRAPHS BY SONJA BULLATY AND ANGELO LOMEO

The distance from Sonora in northern Mexico to arctic Canada is 2,500 miles. A traveler making this long northward march would encounter a remarkable range of vegetation, from the low, stubborn shrubs of the arid south, through the luxuriant forests of northern America, to the gnarled trees that survive above the Arctic Circle. But such a journey on foot would take the traveler perhaps half a year.

The same plant life can be seen in a fraction of the time on the western slopes of the Sierra Nevada. Each 1,000 feet a hiker climbs corresponds roughly to a northward advance of 300 miles. As he ascends, he traverses separate realms where the conditions and forms of life are similar to those found en route from Mexico to the Arctic. These belts of mountainside vegetation, five in all, are called life zones, each named after the continental region it ecologically resembles.

Life zones are generally determined by altitude, but several other factors are involved: amount of moisture, kind of soil, exposure to sun and wind. Plants climb higher on southward-facing slopes, which receive up to three times more sunlight than northern slopes.

No single plant is an infallible indicator of a zone. Some plants, such as the Chinese houses, grow in two or more zones; others, like the lilac-hued fireweed, are found all the way from the foothills to the summits. But the zones are usually distinct enough to be broadly recognized.

In the Sierra the journey begins in the foothills—the Upper Sonoran Zone. Here the deep shade cast by groves of live oaks relieves the glare of sun on southern hillsides. The traveler senses a change as he climbs, reaching the Transition Zone at an altitude of several thousand feet. Here the hiker climbs through pine woods that extend all the way through the higher Canadian Zone, which mirrors the tall forests of the north. And when the ground becomes wild and rocky, and the traveler finds himself following the red snow plant along the edge of melting snow, he knows he is in the Hudsonian Zone, named after the Hudson Bay area of Canada.

Finally, in the Arctic-Alpine Zone, the traveler stands amid desolate waves of rock and patches of low-lying greenery. Here yellow alpine columbine huddle for shelter behind a rock—precisely as they do in the Arctic, 2,000 miles away.

This single photograph, taken in the Mount Stewart area, displays all five life zones of the western Sierra slope. The angle of view and the distortion of the photographer's lens have condensed distance and perspective: the actual boundaries of the zones are separated by several thousand feet.

ARCTIC-ALPINE ZONE

HUDSONIAN ZONE

CANADIAN ZONE

TRANSITION ZONE

UPPER SONORAN ZONE

Upper Sonoran Zone: Life in a Dry Climate

Life is not easy for the plants that grow along the valley margins and up the steep, grassy Sierran foothills between 500 and 5,000 feet. After the March rains the sun burns down until well into October, drying and cracking the earth. The rains return in November, but they are meager. There is little snow to soak the ground as it melts.

In this zone, two distinct plant communities intermingle: woodland and chaparral. Chaparral is a dense, thorny shrub, growing in clumps five to eight feet tall. Sometimes nearly impenetrable, chaparral gave its name to the protective leather leggings—or chaps—worn by cowboys.

Smooth grass and sparse, rounded clusters of trees give the woodland a groomed, parklike appearance. Live oaks, which keep their foliage year round, offer shade; sycamores occasionally mingle with the oaks. But the distinctive tree of the zone —and the first conifer encountered on the western mountain slope—is the digger pine. Gray and thin, the digger pine has few needles, making it virtually shadeless.

This ascetic zone knows one moment of exuberance. Beginning in the lower meadows during March and reaching higher levels by April, there is a profusion of tiny wild flowers *(opposite and overleaf)*. It is a brief extravagance: the flowers wither by the end of May. A lone exception, standing through June, is the tall farewell-to-spring *(bottom right)*.

LIVE OAK AND (RIGHT) CALIFORNIA SYCAMORE

JOHNNY TUCK, OR OWL CLOVER

BABY BLUE-EYES

FAREWELL-TO-SPRING

CALIFORNIA POPPY

MINER'S LETTUCE

VIOLET

FIVE-SPOT

LACEPOD, OR FRINGEPOD

FILAREE

The Transition Zone: A Hospitable Place

Blindfolded, a man could recognize the Transition Zone by the fine music of the yellow pine—or so claimed the naturalist John Muir. In his ranking of forest trees, he placed the yellow, or ponderosa, pine second only to the more majestic sugar pine. But he thought the yellow pine more graceful—and, above all, he liked the hum of the wind through its needles.

This pine, which grows to a height of 200 feet, is the dominant tree of the Transition Zone, outnumbering white firs, shapely trees that have soft green needles growing in fanlike arrangements. The yellow pine gets its name from the striking color of its bark, which is divided by deep grooves into massive plates, five feet long and up to 20 inches wide.

A hospitable climate marks the Transition Zone, which descends down to 1,200 feet in places on the western slopes and reaches up to 9,000 feet on some southern exposures. Summers here are warm and dry, winters cool and snowy, supplying up to 80 inches of precipitation a year. The combination of summer warmth and winter moisture supports a fine array of flowers, shown opposite and on the next two pages. Meadows are replete with shooting stars, their petals bent back as if in swift motion. The heavily scented mountain misery carpets the open spaces. The Miwok Indians used an infusion made from the mountain misery's pungent leaves as a cure-all and called the plant *kit-kit-dizze.*

YELLOW (PONDEROSA) PINE; WHITE FIR (LEFT BACKGROUND)

SHOOTING STAR

LUPINE

COW PARSNIP

MOUNTAIN MISERY

MUSTANG CLOVER

LARKSPUR

CRANESBILL GERANIUM

MARIPOSA LILY

MULE EARS

The Canadian Zone: A Cool Realm

As plants are found higher up on the mountains, their forms are drawn with increasing elegance and economy. An example is the tall, sober red fir of the Canadian Zone. This striking tree grows to a height of 175 feet with a trunk up to five feet thick, and its purplish-red bark tints the forests a rusty hue. Its branches grow downward, then up in swooping, graceful arcs, with long purplish cones at their tips.

Although the red fir seems to be the natural master of this zone, the lodgepole pine shares predominance. The lodgepole is a smaller, slenderer tree, 80 feet tall with a trunk often only 10 inches thick. With their shorter stature and their thin, wrinkled bark, they look like footmen to the lordly red firs.

In the Canadian Zone, which extends up to 10,000 feet on southern slopes, summers are cool, winters cold, and from November to May heavy snow blankets the ground. The flowers shown on the opposite page bloom in turns after the snow has melted. The first is the bright red snow plant. Since this plant does not have green leaves it cannot use sunlight to manufacture food by photosynthesis, as do most plants; instead it feeds on decayed organic matter through its root system. In July, the corn lily appears, and in August and September, tiger lilies spring up near the mountain streams, looking more like jaguars than tigers—if one can imagine orange jaguars.

RED FIR (FOREGROUND) AND LODGEPOLE PINE

YELLOW MONKEY FLOWER

CORN LILY

CAMAS

BOYKINIA

SNOW PLANT

TIGER LILY

The Hudsonian Zone: Region of Change

There is an aura of suspense in the Sierra at the upper altitudes where the ground turns to rock and plants are few. This is the true beginning of the high Sierra, the edge of another world—the Hudsonian Zone (or Subalpine Belt), which extends down from timber line to the boundaries of the forests below. Summer days here are warm, but the nights are always chilly. Plants have three months in which to grow, but though they have adapted to sharp temperature changes frost may kill a few at any moment. The survivors, understandably, have a delicate and withdrawn look.

The wet soils of this area support red heather, which grows soon after the melting of the heavy snows. In June and July the Indian paintbrush, a parasite on the roots of other plants, sprouts thin, tubular flowers. Mats of stonecrop soften the ground. A few misty, pagodalike Chinese houses reach from the foothills and forests up to these heights.

Whitebark pine grows in the rockiest areas of the Hudsonian Zone. This tree, like its northern counterpart, the foxtail pine, grows along the timber line on exposed barren ground; it bears dark cones and blue-green needles cluster at the tips of branches. As the tree climbs the mountain it shrinks, stoops and finally prostrates itself before harsh winds and heavy snows; at timber line, it is a tangle of gnarled branches sprawled over the rock.

RED HEATHER

STONECROP

CHINESE HOUSES

INDIAN PAINTBRUSH

WHITEBARK PINE

The Arctic-Alpine Zone: The Edge of Subsistence

Whoever climbs to the summits of the Sierra will know why prophets have always sought mountaintops to commune with their gods. A strong, clear light falls on a frozen tableau: massive rock on massive rock with scattered lakelets to interrupt the vast cold emptiness.

The few plants that live in the Arctic-Alpine Zone (or Alpine Belt) have had to adapt to cruel conditions. A permanent wind blows, sometimes more than 120 miles an hour. Temperature varies widely (even on a summer evening, it may fall to 28°). It seldom rains and most of the snow is blown away by the wind. The thin soil is granite dust, which sheds the rare water too quickly. Intense solar radiation poses the constant threat of dehydration.

Yet the plants survive. They ignore the wind by hugging the ground and hiding behind rocks. They preserve heat with such thick and closely knit foliage that the interiors of plant clusters are sometimes 20° warmer than the air. Against dehydration they have adopted many of the structures of desert plants. Deep, wide rootstalks store food and water. Small leathery leaf surfaces are equipped with hairs or glands to preserve moisture. Between the chinks in all this protective armor come the surprisingly delicate flowers shown at right. Clad in gentle colors, looking almost frivolous in this stark and naked landscape, they are a poignant tribute to the tenacity of life.

FIREWEED

WALLFLOWER

PRICKLY PHLOX

YELLOW ALPINE COLUMBINE AND SIERRAN ROCK

4/ Four Sierra Creatures

Coyotes…are beautiful animals, and, although cursed by man, are beloved of God. Their sole fault is that they are fond of mutton.   JOHN MUIR/ AT SMOKEY JACK'S SHEEP CAMP

The animal life of the high Sierra is quite sparse compared to that in more hospitable wildernesses such as the subtropical Everglades or in the lush rain forest of the Olympic Peninsula. Here in the Sierra, the wild things are, as the Sequoia ranger said, "right on the margin of existence, hanging on." Like that ranger, I cannot help but marvel at them, and the ways in which they adapt and survive. Among the denizens of the high country are four creatures that I find particularly intriguing.

THE PREDATOR/I first heard the voice of the coyote on a night in the northern Sierra when a harvest moon had just risen to touch the ridges above Alta Morris Lake in the heart of Desolation Wilderness. The night was cold, with gusts from the sundown wind buffeting the tents where the others were already sleeping after a long day in the saddle. I had stayed up, close to the pine-knot fire, to watch the moon. The wild creatures, too, were out with the moon, the predators ranging in the extra light; and some time after midnight, from the passes and along the meadows and draws, the coyotes began to call. The first sound was a single cry, high and far off and inexpressibly wild. It was like that of a wolf, but more contralto, and broken at the end into a series of shrill-toned barkings as though the coyote had run after his own howl and bitten it into small pieces. A second coyote answered the call. Then another and another took up the cry until our campground was wholly circled within

a distant ring of primeval sound that lasted through half a waking hour.

In my next incarnation, when I hear that sound I will take up my knife or my stone ax and go out to hunt with my wild brothers. For their calling stirred something deep and quick inside me. It made me think then as I have ever since of the coyotes as my brothers, just as the boy Mowgli in Kipling's *Jungle Book* knew the wolves to be his brothers when he sat with them in a ring in the moonlight as they uttered the jungle cry, "We be of one blood, thou and I." But as a city animal bred away from the wild ways, the best I could do for now was go to my sleeping bag and curl up much too safe and warm, listening to the quavering signals of the unseen coyotes on the chase and feeling distinctly left out. I saw my first coyote only a few days later, some distance south of Desolation on a wooded plateau above Yosemite Valley. Again it was early evening, the hour when the midday heat is spent and the coyotes find the prowling more congenial among the cooling rocks and meadows. As I moved along a road a grayish full-ruffed animal loped from the edge of a stand of white fir. His feet were tiny, his legs slender, his gait rhythmic and long and light as that of any ballerina. In his mouth he carried a squirrel that he had just taken. He gave me a short, appraising glance in the manner of coyotes, to see if I was threatening or edible, decided I was neither and ran another 150 yards in the open without looking again, to disappear finally into the shadows of a manzanita thicket.

The sight of the coyote was almost as moving as the sound had been, and nothing like the image of the scroungy, skulking barnyard cutthroat that is the coyote of almost any tale ever told by a sheepherder or cattle rancher. Stockmen hate the coyote with the same fearful passion that early settlers and their European forebears turned on the wolf. The popular notion has always been that all coyotes are sheep killers, calf slayers and chicken thieves. A senior biologist in the Department of Agriculture once called him "the arch-predator of our times," deserving no mercy. The coyote is also cursed of hunters as a mortal threat to the good little soft-eyed creatures of the forest, i.e., wild animals and birds that do not compete with predatory man and that taste good to the man who kills them. As a result, the federal government in 1915 joined the several states in a coyote pogrom that in 32 years wiped out 1,884,897 coyotes across the country; California was one of the leaders in the vintage killing years. The fact that the slaughter made very little ecological or economic sense (in 1962 the federal program spent $90,-195 in California to kill coyotes that had eaten $3,501 worth of sheep)

did nothing to deter the trappers and poisoners. They went right on killing, not just coyotes but all effective predators: the last grizzly bear in California was reported seen in 1924, the last wolf disappeared from the Sierra about the same time, and the most recent count put the Sierra mountain lion population at 150.

Now, in effect, only the coyote is left; and he has his hands full. For nature put predators on earth for good reasons. Without them the land is much the worse, and so are the men on it—not to mention the soft-eyed forest creatures. Coyotes do indeed pull down an occasional deer. But in so doing they keep the herd strong. A healthy, full-grown deer, with its slashing hoofs, is a match for any coyote. Therefore the coyote takes old, weak or diseased deer or winnows out the fawns. As a result, the herds do not grow so large they overbrowse their winter range to the point of subsequent massive starvation.

Coyotes also kill millions of rabbits, hares, ground squirrels, gophers and other small rodents, furry small fry that make up half the average coyote's diet. In regions where men have killed off predators like the rodent-eating coyotes, their erstwhile victims have nibbled the valleys and meadows bare and pocked the ground with so many tunnels and den holes that any horse or cow still interested in the denuded pasture is in real danger of breaking a leg.

Another fourth of the coyote's food is carrion, which someone ought to be cleaning up. And the remainder is a copious but economically inconsequential gallimaufry of grasshoppers and other large insects, mesquite beans, cherries, tadpoles, frogs, stranded fish, snakes (which a coyote will tease like a mongoose before killing), watermelon, juniper and manzanita berries, crayfish, apples, plastic surveyor's tape, duck eggs, garbage, old shoes and bits of leather harness, ducks (which the coyote sometimes catches by swimming beneath the water and grabbing a diving duck by the head), wild rose hips and almost anything else he can chew or swallow.

The Indians and early Mexicans, being in harmony with the land and its wild animals, knew all this and had feelings of great warmth toward the coyote. The *vaqueros* called him *amigo,* and learned to sing back and forth with him when he called at night. They claimed they could understand coyote talk: high-pitched yips meant good weather; deep tones foretold snow. Some Indians even worshiped him. Apaches believed they would become coyotes in the afterlife, a transfiguration I, for one, would be delighted to share. To the Miwoks the coyote was a god who

A mountain coyote finds his food supply reduced by early winter snows. Cold weather drives much small game into hibernation, but the omnivorous coyotes can make a meal of practically anything from berries to a discarded boot. They seldom descend below the 4,500-foot level except in the worst weather, and then only briefly.

modeled man in clay, breathed life into him at dawn and cried out in joy
—as he still does at that time of day.

My own feelings toward the coyote are, as you may have gathered,
somewhere between the Indians' spiritualistic worship and an ordinary
wilderness traveler's plain admiration. I admire the coyote as an at-
tentive family man (although like even a human husband he may
occasionally stray) who sometimes brings food to his pregnant wife,
plays with the pups when the mother lets him near them—which is not
often—teaches them to hunt as they get older, helps to move them to a
new den if he senses a mountain lion or a man on the prowl, and af-
fectionately touches noses with wife or friends when he meets them
after returning from a long hunt.

I admire, too, his marvelous speed and endurance. One coyote was
clocked at close to 50 miles per hour in a short burst, others have been
known to hold 30 or 35 for a full five miles; and in a season when the
pickings are lean a coyote may range for 125 miles in a single hunt. His
ingenuity is simply awesome. He seems to know exactly where in a shallow tunnel a pocket gopher or a deer mouse will be. Going after a hare,
which can outrun him on a flat, the coyote hunts with a partner that
lies in ambush until the hare is chased past a prearranged point. If the
prey is a succulent but wary bird such as a goose, several coyotes may
dance and cavort at an apparently harmless distance from the fascinated bird while a confederate creeps up from the other direction. At
bumblebee nests the coyote will wave his tail until all the curious or ir-
ritated bees have swarmed out, then stick in his nose and eat the honey.
He will follow deer-, duck- and quail-shooters, knowing he will get
more than his share of cripples. In the snow time he will stand near a
bull elk as it paws through the snow for grass, aware that the hoofs
will also turn up field mice. And he will even adopt a road-grading
crew so he can stand down-field from the bulldozer and wait as it
scrapes up earth—and everything that lives therein.

His courage is fierce and tends to be selfless. He will present himself
as a lure to distract men or hounds from chasing his pups, and he will
try to support physically a gunshot comrade to get him away from the
hunters. Caught in a steel trap, he will drag the device for miles, sometimes managing to catch a gopher or two en route. And if he cannot
shake loose from the trap jaws, his will to freedom is so strong that he
may gnaw off his own paw to get loose.

As for his killing of domestic animals, I find it hard to censure the coy-

ote for pulling down calves, mainly because he rarely does so. For one thing, the presence of even the most sluggardly and inattentive mother cow is likely to keep a coyote at a respectful distance. For another, stockmen tend to attribute all their losses to predators, whether or not there is a coyote within 100 miles. And finally, coyotes just do not seem very interested: a naturalist once saw a shaky little calf walk up and sniff at a coyote who was hunting field mice. The hungry coyote simply growled as might any busy adult at an intrusive child, and that was the end of the encounter.

It is quite true that some coyotes like mutton, and even better, lamb. But this kind of predation seems confined to a few tough individuals, just as burglary is the modus vivendi of only certain kinds of humans. In sheep country during the lambing season, when the pickings are most lush, the stomachs of only 15 per cent of trapped or shot coyotes showed sheep remains—and some of these remains were certainly carrion. The solution to the problem of the few sheep killers is to identify them, as has been done in many cases, and leave the others alone, since they usually pass up lamb dinner for grasshoppers or berries or other low-hazard food.

If it is necessary to discuss chicken stealing at all, let us not be surprised that, since we have driven the coyote out of the most productive range land, he comes back once in a while to knock over a fat pullet.

Happily, both the state of California and the major federal agencies that function there are coming to a much more benevolent, enlightened attitude toward the coyote. "Our own Department went out of the predator control business some time ago," says one California Fish and Game man. The U.S. Park and Forest Service people rarely go after coyotes, and are becoming less and less happy when others do so. A few ranchers still shoot coyotes on sight; and private trappers continue to take coyotes, which they sell on the fur market as "arctic fox" or "baby wolf." But these residual coyote killers are getting little official encouragement. In fact, the most enlightened agencies most recently have become downright protective toward their coyotes, since every historical lesson shows that when predators are taken out, deer and rodents spread like a plague.

"I think," says one ranger, "we're getting farther and farther away from the concept of good animals, like the deer and squirrels and such, and bad animals—the predators. I don't think it's our job to define good and bad that way. As we and the public get more educated about these things, we're learning to enjoy *all* wildlife. Besides," he added, in

a moment of great illumination, "how can we say good or bad anyway, unless we do it in terms of man?"

His question challenges the historic attitude toward predators. And the fact that a responsible official was ready to ask the question suggests that at long, staggering last, 20th Century white man is beginning to move away from his ancient concept of a self-centered ecology. If he keeps moving, he may one day become as wise as the Indians. But he will never be so wise as my brother, the coyote.

THE BIRD/It would be awful to be called something as silly as an ouzel (pronounced *oo-z'l*), unless you were an oblivious, good-natured sort of clown who did not seem aware of what people were saying about him. Clearly this is the life style of the water ouzel, a slate-gray bird that, like the deadpan comic Buster Keaton, proceeds with stoic energy and unruffled mien to do everything wrong—and thrive. He is by some distance my favorite of all Sierra birds. Partly this is because he does indeed remind me of Buster Keaton, of whom I have been a lifelong fan. And partly it is because, with the exception of hawks and eagles whose power and purpose I admire, I tend to regard most birds as basically rather silly. The ouzel, being the silliest, is therefore a favorite.

First of all, he does not seem wholly aware of the fact that he is a bird, although he looks something like a wren. He seems mixed up about what birds do: fly in the air, build nests in quiet places, pull worms from the earth. The ouzel builds his nest in the wettest and noisiest place imaginable, behind a waterfall or right next to the edge of a cascade. Though each nest is a brilliant piece of architecture, it does not look like a nest at all, but more like a beehive or a Watutsi hut. Dome-shaped with a single arched doorway, it is made of pieces of green moss so fresh and so tightly woven that they continue to grow even after the nest is finished. From this soggy but elegant headquarters the ouzel sallies forth to look for food, which he does almost exclusively at the bottoms of pools and running streams.

At first glance the ouzel seems wholly unequipped for such underwater work, having neither webbed feet for swimming nor the shovel bill that helps most water birds dredge up their dinner. The ouzel usually feeds in the shallows, sitting on a stone and bobbing his head under every three or four seconds to turn over pebbles and rocks for the insect larvae that cling beneath. If that does not work, he flutters to midstream and dives straight to the bottom, where he walks upright on his clawed feet for a minute or more, calmly poking around just as

A bird that can fly underwater, an ouzel prepares for one of its curious stream-bottom strolls in search of food. Ouzel fancier John Muir described the bird as "a singularly joyous and lovable little fellow as smoothly plump and compact as a pebble that has been whirled in a pothole."

though he were plucking seeds from a lawn. During such submarine forays, the ouzel closes a scaly trap door over each nostril to keep water from coming in. At the same time he protects his eyes by lowering over them a filmy membrane that, like a skin-diver's mask, keeps the water from interfering with his vision.

If the current is flowing fast, as it usually is in ouzel country, the bird walks upstream so that his beak and head deflect the current and his whole body is often encased in a clear bubble of subsurface air. And whenever the rushing stream becomes too powerful for the ouzel to keep his feet, he simply spreads his wings and begins to fly underwater, perfectly sure that this is a sensible activity.

Unlike most other birds, the ouzel is not concerned with variations in the weather, no matter how violent. His relatives in Alaska and Asia dive into cascades when the thermometer is at 50 below. In the Sierra at 11,000 feet in a mid-January blizzard, with four feet of snow already on the ground and the open streams a mass of snow sludge and ice shards, the ouzel, bobbing about looking for frozen bugs, will be as happy as if it were the height of summer.

Occasionally the ouzel gets around to behaving like ordinary birds, but not very much like them and not very often. As birds will do, he preens himself by plucking oil with his bill from a gland at the base of his tail and lubricating his feathers. But the ouzel does so on a heroic scale, being something of an aquatic superman; he has an oil gland 10 times larger than that of land birds his size to enable him to waterproof his feathers. Sometimes the ouzel actually flies in the air. But whenever he does so he tries to stay directly over a stream, following every bend, rising and dipping over rapids in a course parallel to the contours of the water. At a waterfall he will go into an abrupt power dive down the falls to the bottom, where he levels off just over the water.

Perhaps the most startling thing of all about this bizarre and homely little creature is his song. It is perfectly lovely, a pure sequence of melodic trills with a tone somewhere between a flute and a clarinet. As he does everything else, the ouzel sings where and when he chooses, even in the teeth of a winter gale. And he does it with a style and assurance indicating that he is totally certain—even if nobody else is—that any ouzel is not only a proper bird in his own right, but very likely the best of all possible birds.

THE FISH/I never felt badly about killing a fish until I caught my first golden trout. Up to that point I had the conventional American attitude to-

Collecting food for winter, a pika carries grass to dry in its rockslide shelter.

A marmot pauses between quick mouthfuls to scan the horizon for enemies.

Mottled fur camouflages a California ground squirrel.

The Rodents' Dangerous World

In the Sierra, as in most other places, the rodents lead all the orders of mammals both in numbers and in diversity. Their multitudinous ranks include hibernators (marmots), non-hibernators (rabbits), tree dwellers (flying squirrels), burrow diggers (aplodontia), nut eaters (chipmunks) and grass eaters (pikas), insect and meat eaters (grasshopper mice), and many species that will settle for eating almost anything if their preferred food supply fails.

Different as the species are, most share the rodent characteristic of curved, prominent front teeth that continue growing throughout their lives. Tireless gnawing or chewing keeps these specialized teeth filed down to sharp cutting edges. The constant filing is vital: If a beaver somehow is prevented from gnawing off branches for his dam, his rodent incisors grow until they lock his jaws shut, and starvation follows.

The rodents also have in common a casualty rate high enough to counterbalance their fecundity. Small and defenseless, they serve by the thousands as staples or snacks in the diet of local predators, furred, feathered or scaly. If predators did not find them so attractive, the prolific voles, two-ounce mouselike creatures that bear several litters of three to seven young each year, might well overpopulate their meadowland habitat.

A tiny Belding ground squirrel squats on its haunches to peer over low grasses.

ward fish as fair game to anyone with hunger pangs or an impulse for low-risk sport. My first encounter with a golden came on one of those superb frost-cold Sierra mornings along Rock Creek near the headwaters of the Kern River. The sun was too bright and, by the time I was fully organized, already too high for good fishing. But we had time to burn. A planned trail ride was delayed by the nocturnal departure of two of our mules and one horse, whose tracks indicated they had wandered toward their home corral. The packer grumpily started after them at dawn, muttering through mouthfuls of canned peaches about the ancestry, morals and I.Q. of all livestock. I decided to use the hour or two of his travail by taking a walk alongside the creek with my rod and a handful of splendid little flies tied to order by a Connecticut neighbor's son after he had done much research into the particular entomology of this very corner of the mountains.

The walk in itself was delightful. At each bend and riffle the creek subtly changed the low, chuckling tone of its voice. I moved downstream to a place where a waterfall had carved a perfect pool—deep water with a rock in the middle where a trout could lie still, out of the current, then flicker off to strike at whatever food might float into sight.

I fished the pool carefully, staying in the shade as much as possible, squatting down on my heels to cast so as not to throw a disturbing shadow into any fish's line of sight. After perhaps an hour I managed to drop a caddisfly right at the bottom of the falls, so that it swirled in a natural manner just past the rock and perhaps six inches under the water. A shadow darted out and I felt a delicate, almost subliminal touch on the line. By happy chance I was raising the rod tip for another cast, so the hook set.

In perhaps three minutes I had the fish ashore. It was 10½ inches long, its back and tail a glistening olive green, the body shading from yellow to rich gold along the sides to vermilion down the center of the belly. The gill covers gleamed bright red, as did the lower fins, with an added touch of white along the edges. The tailfin, dorsal and entire back were speckled with black dots, while oval patches of gray punctuated the golden side strips. The trout was as striking in color as many tropical fish, far too handsome to be yanked out of the water for someone's breakfast; and I immediately wished that the creature were back swimming free beneath the falls. Unfortunately, the hook had set deeply in the mouth cartilage, which I tore in trying to disengage the fly; there was no purpose in returning the crippled fish to the water. I there-

fore took it back to the campground and showed it to the ranger with whom I was riding.

He told me the golden was a separate species of trout *(Salmo agua-bonita),* native only to the Kern Plateau in the southern Sierra Nevada. The species had evolved sometime after the Pleistocene when volcanic upheavals changed water flow to isolate a number of rainbow or cut-throat trout (there is debate about which species was involved) in the creeks of the granite tableland south of Mount Whitney. There, either by coincidence or by the natural adjustment of protective coloration, the fish slowly took on the hues of the yellow volcanic sediments and reddish granite sand in the stream-bed gravel.

Thus, old-school Sierra watchers claim the golden is a Kern River rainbow once removed. Superficially it seems to be, since the golden hybridizes freely with the rainbow to produce fertile young, and its native waters once flowed gently into the Kern before the volcanic activity along the stream beds created cascades the fish could not negotiate.

The first goldens ever to journey outside the Kern Plateau made the trip in a coffeepot carried in 1876 by a lumberman who dumped them into the Cottonwood Creek drainage where he hoped they would provide him with good sport as he worked his nearby sawmill. They did, and their progeny have since supplied superb fishing through much of the Sierra and wherever else they have been planted, for the Cottonwood Lakes, under the loving eye of the California Department of Fish and Game, have become a golden trout breeding ground. Each year the department takes upward of 700,000 eggs to incubate and then sow as baby fish in some 150 lakes and streams.

The goldens, whether Kern Plateau natives or transplants, are the fussiest, subtlest feeders of any fish I have encountered. And while this characteristic provides just the sort of masochistic pleasure a fly fisher dotes on, it makes the golden a poor competitor for food against such other immigrant species as the brown and the eastern brookie with which he may find himself sharing a pool. For this reason, as well as the golden's deplorable habit of hybridizing with the rainbow into a demispecies, the department has become more and more selective about where it drops its goldens, and chary of allowing other species to invade established golden trout habitats. Lately the department has tried to maintain some waters in the high Sierra as pure golden territory, temporarily poisoning invaded drainage systems and then replanting them with golden fingerlings.

The department has given further protection to the golden, from man

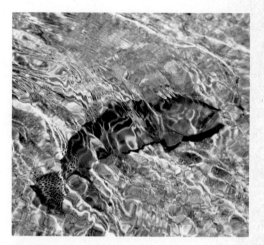

Basking in a Sierra stream, a golden trout enjoys cold, well-aerated waters at elevations of 8,000 feet or more. A native of the southerly region of the Kern Plateau, the golden was unknown in the northern lakes and streams it now populates until anglers started to stock those waters in the 1870s.

A mountain lion patrols its well-defined territory, hunting for game and repelling invaders throughout an area of up to 125 square miles.

A Last Stronghold for the Big Cats

The mountain lion in action is a model of graceful ferocity; in an age when predators were widely hated, Theodore Roosevelt called the species "the lord of stealthy murder." The big cats (frequently called cougars) weigh as much as 225 pounds. They creep up silently on their prey and then explode from ambush in a short, swift charge. They are powerful enough to kill a 200-pound mule deer with a single bite and to drag the carcass upslope for miles to their rocky lair.

The lion's much maligned role as a predator explains why it is rarely seen in the Sierra today. In 1907 California's mule deer, which supply about 75 per cent of the cougar's diet, were dangerously depleted by human hunters; in a misguided effort to help the herds regain normal size, the Division of Fish and Game offered a bounty on mountain lions. In 56 years, $388,730 was paid out for the killing of 12,461 of them. As a result, the state's lion population now stands at an estimated 600, with only 150 spread out through the vast reaches of the Sierra.

Yet according to one study, a mature lion eats only one deer a week. The Sierra mountain lion probably never had much effect on the local deer population. Because the war on lions has not helped the deer, the state bounty was repealed in 1963. Nevertheless, there still is no law protecting the endangered big cats, which may be hunted in season.

A snow-spattered cougar pauses in the hunt.

this time, by forbidding all angling in four of the 13 Cottonwood Lakes and by lowering daily catch limits in the remaining lakes and feeder streams; the limit has dropped from the standard 10 to a more modest five. Several years ago Inyo National Forest ecologists drew up a plan, still under consideration, to reclassify and rename part of the Kern region as the Golden Trout Wilderness. One of the planners, an ichthyologist and a key man in the maintenance of the Sierra as a sport fishery, suggests the day may come when the golden trout receives the same no-kill immunity that all national parks animals now enjoy.

"When I was a kid," he says, "there was a willow bush by this one stream where I could catch all the fish I wanted in an hour. Now my kids are happy if they catch one or two. And I can see this philosophy extended to the point where people may think of the golden as something to catch and admire and put back, rather than eat."

I applaud this reasoning, both as a sporting proposition and as a matter of gastronomics. I prefer the taste of brook trout, whose flesh generally strikes me as being firmer and moister. I suspect, however, that there are those who will disagree with this judgment. And I am certain there will be shouts of rage at any throwback rule imposed in the high Sierra, where at least 75 per cent of back-country visitors carry flyrods or spinning gear. But this majority of anglers may have an even greater shock ahead.

"Eventually," adds the ichthyologist in a burst of purism that even a part-time bumbler like me finds a bit extreme, "we may not catch the golden at all but just look at them and appreciate them as a living part of the wilderness."

THE MONARCH MANQUÉ/In the world of people it is seldom that the most attractive man is both a posturing male chauvinist and a gauche lover. But among the animals of the Sierra, this is most certainly the case. In all the high country there is no creature more striking, more regal than the California bighorn, or mountain sheep. A fully developed ram may stand 35 inches at the shoulder and weigh up to 250 pounds; his magnificently curved horns, nearly five inches thick at the base, sweep through arcs that may be a yard around and bring the total weight of the animal's head to as much as 30 pounds. Unlike the mule deer, which sheds his antlers each year, the mountain sheep carries his horns all his life. They first appear as buttons on his head when he is a lamb of three months. They keep growing up and back and then down and forward until at the 12th or 14th year they enclose a full circle. A

ram thus adorned carries his head very erect, as though inordinately proud of his masculine crown. But the fact is, the horns weigh so much he has to learn to hold his head just so, adjusting his posture as his horns grow, or he might lose balance and fall while running.

Like so much else about the bighorn, his running is a thing of pure beauty, especially when he is moving among the ledges and crags of the apparently suicidal terrain that is his natural habitat. He travels in summer at altitudes of 10,000 to 14,494 feet (the summit height of Mount Whitney), along the eastern crest of the Sierra, plunging at a full gallop through country where a hiker or even an experienced mountaineer would creep with a rope and a prayer. The bighorn can scramble down a 150-foot cliff in a matter of seconds, half jumping and half tumbling from one tiny ledge to another six, eight or 10 feet below with no hesitant reconnoitering. And he can go back up again almost as fast, grabbing onto the rock with broad, flexible hoofs equipped with a special rubbery pad.

Moving across loose rock on an avalanche slope, the sheep relies on a superb sense of timing. A naturalist once saw a band of 14 bighorn, including three rams, running along a headwall at the top of a canyon toward a 60-degree chute filled with the unstable jumble of loose rocks called talus. As the first bighorn approached the chute on solid rock he put on a burst of speed that let him almost float across the talus with lightning-quick scrambling strides until he bounded onto solid footing on the other side. The sheep crossed one at a time and in a line so that none would be hit by rocks dislodged by another from above. And as each animal made it he turned to wait until the entire band was safely across the chute.

Such sightings of the bighorn are rare. For along with the mountain lion and the wolverine, the mountain sheep is about the hardest of all Sierra animals for a wilderness traveler to see. This is in part because man's historical reaction to the bighorn has been to shoot him, close to the point of wiping out the species. Bighorn meat is very good indeed. One mine cook reported killing 50 bighorn all by himself in the winter of 1895—a dozen years, incidentally, after a moratorium was called on bighorn shooting in California to prevent the extermination of the already hard-pressed species. Today the California bighorn is on the federal list of 157 rare or endangered species. There are fewer than 8,000 bighorn sheep of all species in the whole United States, as compared to an estimated two million in 1800. And of this remnant, only 215 California bighorn survive in the Sierra, scattered in small

Rams of the Mount Baxter bighorn herd gather in an unusual crowd scene while on the way to their winter range in Inyo National Forest.

bands between Olanche Peak in the south and the Mount Baxter-Sawmill Pass area in the north.

Besides being few in number and fond of impossible terrain, the bighorn is also hard to spot because of his coloration and deliberate caution. His hair and horns are a dun color, the precise shade of the granite country he inhabits. When grazing he moves in studied slow motion, instinctively aware that quick movement catches the eye of any prowler. Between snacks he lies curled up and still in a shallow depression pawed from the earth, looking for all the world like just another granite boulder. I have never seen a bighorn in the Sierra, although I have seen their tracks in the granite sand of a broad alpine barren some 12 miles northwest of Mount Whitney. I have no doubt, however, that they have seen me. Few creatures on earth have better eyesight than the mountain sheep. Another naturalist, studying a band of sheep so far away he had to use eight-power field glasses, noted that whenever he made the slightest movement every sheep in the band—made up mainly of ewes and lambs—would instantly raise its head to look even though the observer's clothes blended in color with the rock against which he was standing. If she is sure she has been seen and lacks an escape route, a ewe will sometimes place her body between the observer—who represents peril—and her lamb.

It would rarely occur to a ram to do such a thing. In fact, rams are rotten fathers. As noted earlier, they are the worst kind of male chauvinists, with a powerful sense of themselves and a penchant for traveling in privacy-seeking bachelor bands. They seldom, if ever, spend time with the lambs they have sired or with the ewes that bore their progeny—except when it is time to mate. Alas, when his great moment of mating arrives, the lordly bighorn ram becomes a posturing, bumbling high-country buffoon.

The mating, or rutting, season in the Sierra starts in late October, whenever the first ewe happens to come into heat. As that occurs the rams lose all interest in bachelor living and start chasing girls with great enthusiasm but not necessarily much success. When a feeding ram catches the scent of a ewe in heat his head snaps up and he stretches his neck forward with the nose straight out and his head tipping steadily from side to side. Usually two or more rams pick up the smell simultaneously. Then they set out after the lady at a fast trot. They bowl over any animal between them and their intended, stumble boorishly on stones, sometimes on their knees but never stopping.

If the object of all this confusion is an older ewe, she may stand around and wait for the gentlemen to arrive. A younger ewe will often take off at top speed.

Meanwhile the rams, whose amorous impulses seem not only gauche but frequently short-lived, may turn away from the ewe to square off in a ritualistic and almost totally harmless joust. For openers there is a good deal of groaning and snorting and milling about between two rams. This can last for a couple of hours, and were it to occur between combatants at a modern prize fight or an ancient tournament at arms, the crowd would be bored silly. To the intent rams, however, it is all part of the mandatory facedown.

From time to time during these preliminaries the rams will approach each other and, standing head to rump, one ram tries with his forefoot to hit the other in the genitals. Whether or not either party is scored upon, there is no evasive action taken nor any indication of pain or irritation. When the kicking is over, a brief period of camaraderie follows, with much licking of each other's sides—whereupon the erstwhile combatants amble off to feed. However they keep a close eye on each other, signaling ceremonial ferocity by pawing the ground and giving off a few more snorts. Suddenly, as though upon a silent signal, both will rear, their front legs flailing the air. Then they drop onto all fours, apparently to get fully set. Finally they rear once more, draw a bead on each other down their noses and charge at top speed with heads lowered to crash together with a BONK that is audible for three quarters of a mile. The collision, occurring at speeds from 50 to 70 mph, generates an impact that has been estimated at 2,400 pounds; from which the immediate effect upon the rams is usually zero, though a lifetime of such jousting can scar their horns deeply.

They just stand there a moment, then back off and go at it again. This sometimes continues on and off all afternoon, with about five-minute intervals between charges until the two swains have had as many as 40 brain-rattling collisions. At no time during a charge does either one so much as think of chickening out. On the contrary, they aim and time their rushes to create dead-on collisions, and if one ram chances to lean a little to the side, the other leans to compensate. Meanwhile the ewe has long since wandered away from all this manly assertion to feed by herself, massively unimpressed by the show. In the special world of the bighorn, it would not matter if she stayed around. For the rams, particularly in the preliminary stages of the rut,

appear much more interested in dueling than in love-making. The jousts have no outcome in terms of victor or vanquished. The rams just stop banging heads after a while. If the lady is still around, neither one may get her or both may give it a try. Either way the preliminaries of actual courtship and sometimes the attempt itself are so brief that it is small wonder the ewes soon wander off—or flee.

Somehow the species has managed to weather an eon of such posturing gracelessness at the mating game. But it has barely managed to survive the onslaught of man into its habitat. Even though the legal shooting of sheep ended almost a hundred years ago and poaching in the Sierra is now negligible, there are simply too many people trampling through the bighorn's terrain. All the Sierra sheep live within the Inyo National Forest and the eastern fringe of Sequoia National Park, where total recreational visitors increased from a quarter of a million in 1950 to well over two million in 1971. The presence of all these people has made the bighorn skittish and recessive, pushed onto ranges where survival is more difficult than in their normal, more congenial habitat. During the 1950s and 1960s the California bighorn sheep population declined by almost 45 per cent as the animals retreated into the most barren and remote corners to get away.

Fortunately the forest and park officials have noted the threat of human intrusion and have begun to do something about it. There is a firm plan to build no new foot or horse trails into sheep country, and the trails presently there are being allowed to erode away. Within a few years overnight camping in sheep country will probably be prohibited, permits will be required to enter at all, and travel will be restricted to certain very limited areas. Thus the bighorn will be encouraged in his preposterous romantic ways, to the continued survival of the species, and the boredom of the lady sheep.

A Walk along McGee Creek

PHOTOGRAPHS BY DAVID CAVAGNARO

Every mountain stream, like a living creature, has a character all its own. As the stream flows away from the source—a glacier, a lake, a spring or a slow seepage from beneath a rock —it takes its shape and its voice from the land through which it travels. The stream in turn gives to the land the priceless treasure of water, which means life to the growing things along its banks.

In time, the stream on its journey may swell to such power that it re-carves the very face of the mountains where it was born. Or it can remain as fine and delicate as a necklace until, as is the nature of all streams, it finds an ending in a pond or a bog or a larger river. Yet with the ending the stream's existence is not over, for it is continually reborn at its source.

Thus each stream endures as an individual phenomenon and as a lasting fascination to the traveler who chooses to walk beside it and look closely at the things that live there. McGee Creek, high in the central Sierra, provided this fascination for me on one July day's walk. My companion and I encountered McGee Creek around 10 o'clock in the morning at a point in mid-course about 10,400 feet up in McGee Can-

yon, the glaciated basin that gives the creek its source and direction.

The horse trail came down to the stream at a bend where the water flows easily through a small meadow and a copse of lodgepole pine.

At brookside we dismounted, tied up our stirrups and reins, and waved our horses on to loose-herd with the packtrain headed for our campground higher up while we made our acquaintance with the stream.

I was struck at once by the water's richness: here and there beneath the surface the larger rocks were vibrant with coverlets of clean green algae. The splash zone at stream's edge, and the small boggy tables just above, held thriving colonies of mosses; the most intriguing was *Polytrichum* which, in a crucial step of the reproductive cycle, sends out hair-thin stems capped by pods that may hold dozens of spores. These spores hold the key to a remarkable and complicated process that has several stages.

Upon maturing, the spores are scattered by the wind—and the movement of water in the stream —and finally settle in the moist soil and molds near the stream's edge. In time, the spores develop into new green moss plants, each one having

The author's walk along McGee Creek took him through rugged country in the northernmost part of Kings Canyon National Park, shown in the contour map below. He started the hike at a point roughly halfway between the creek's source, the McGee Lakes (dark gray), and its juncture with Evolution Creek (top). He tramped almost three miles upstream, climbing from about 10,400 feet to about 11,000 feet.

McGEE CREEK EMERGING FROM A STAND OF LODGEPOLE PINE AT 10,400 FEET

both male and female sex organs, known as gametophytes. When mature, and if the moss has picked up at least a thin coating of water from the stream, the male and female parts then enter the final step. The male sperm begin to swim through the moist film covering the moss, while the egg-bearing organs emit a sugar that spreads through the adjacent water. The sperm are drawn to the sugar, more powerfully as the concentration increases, until they arrive at the eggs, which then become fertile. The result, in a process that repeats itself until the coming of winter, is a new generation of spore-bearing capsules on the tops of long red stalks.

Mixed in with the moss were stems of wild onion, their roots in

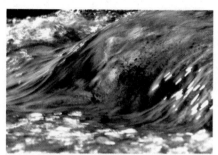

MORNING SUN ON A SMALL RAPID

the boggy ground they prefer, and long strands of sedge. Close by stood the three- to four-foot stalks of corn lilies with their drooping, elongated leaves, and a cluster of delicate Jeffrey shooting stars. Beneath one purple-rimmed blossom a tiny mayfly, with translucent wings folded, was hiding from the wind that was buffeting the catkins of streamside

willow and shaking golden streamers of pollen from the overhanging lodgepoles. A sluggish Behr's sulphur butterfly slowly awakened at its perch among the grasses.

Morning—a Mighty Mushroom

Nearby, the base of a lodgepole pine supported an explosion of a mushroom that scientists call *Lentinus lepideus,* known more colorfully as train-wrecker fungus. Reaching sizes up to three feet square, it grows throughout much of the continent on dead conifers or oaks, and is notorious for attacking railroad ties—especially those not treated with creosote—and eventually rotting them to create the threat from which they get their name.

In a patch of ooze water just below the mushroom, the gray, narrow-

THE REPRODUCTIVE SPORES OF POLYTRICHUM MOSS

WAKING: A BEHR'S SULPHUR BUTTERFLY

ly tubular larval cases of stoneflies littered the pine duff on the bottom. The flies deposited their eggs here last summer, and over the winter the eggs hatched into larvae, building these tubular cases as protection from the cold, from prey birds, and perhaps as camouflage (they look rather like tiny sticks).

Late Morning—Haven for a Snake

Within a radius of another three or four paces were half a dozen other species of insects—all food for a garter snake we saw slithering about in the meadow grass a few hundred yards farther upstream. It is surprising, in fact very rare, to see snakes of any kind at these altitudes. They have little time to find a living here, since they fall into a torpor with the first frost in September and then must hibernate through the many months until the weather becomes endurable late the following spring. Also, at timber line and above, there are too few places where a snake can hide from the quick, deadly Cooper hawks, which like nothing better than reptile. In fact, the high country is so hostile and the odds for a snake are so poor that I often wonder why any of them bother to try to live this far up in these mountains.

The answer in this particular case is probably McGee Creek's congenial surroundings. Being on the western side of the Sierra crest, the creek basin receives much more moisture, in the form of both snow and rain, than the parched stream courses on the east slope, which sometimes dry out completely during the summer. High

A TRAIN-WRECKER FUNGUS

ridges to the east, west and south of the stream give some protection from the wind, and yet the valley is wide enough through its middle reaches so that the stream banks get sunshine from 9 or 10 in the morning through late afternoon.

The central portion of McGee Creek itself would be ideal for snakes at almost any altitude. Here the channel widens and occasionally braids into easy meanders. Dozens of small yellow-legged frogs inhabit the margins of these branchlets. And here, as elsewhere throughout its entire length, McGee Creek is alive with immature golden trout, small enough to be snatched from the water by the swift strike of an alert snake. The creek is embraced by a broad meadow full of grass and

AN UNCOMMON GARTER SNAKE

small bogs in which fat insect larvae hatch by the millions. Polliwogs dart about in the backwaters. A garter snake with any degree of enterprise can do a lot better than survive on this rich diet. And if a hawk should skim by, the snake can either hide in the deep meadow grass or, in a real emergency, dive under the stream's waters and stay submerged until the trouble passes.

Noon—a Pine Cone's History

Thus the snake survived, but examples of the inevitability of death and decay (and their relationship to the living) were everywhere. It was a little after noon when we came upon a thoroughly chewed whitebark pine cone, long ago fallen to the ground. It was dotted with penicillium fungus (the same growth that

A BEE FLY SEEKING ITS HOST

is cultivated to make the drug), two kinds of slime mold and a cup fungus. Some time back a mountain creature, probably a raucous, aggressive bird called the Clark nutcracker, had robbed the cone of its nuts. We saw a nutcracker perched on a rock near a whitebark pine; it usually knocks the cones off the tree, and later, using its bill like a combination of pick and crowbar, pries out the sweet green nuts.

At almost every step along the banks was more testimony to the wealth of life by the stream, and of the close connection between water and plants and insects and animals. Each pool held flickering shadows of golden trout, lazily feeding or darting away from our sudden presence, sometimes in such haste and so close

THE CONE OF A WHITEBARK PINE, ITS NUTS EATEN

THE CONSUMER: A CLARK NUTCRACKER

to the surface of the water that their tail and dorsal fins left tiny rumplings of wake.

The feeding fish often worked in circular patterns, drifting out into the stream and down-current; then, just before being sucked into a rapid they would swim up and into the still water again, each fish seeming to wait for the stream to bring him his bite of food—insects such as the caddisflies and their larvae.

In these high altitudes, where permanent running water is rare, each species of streamside plant plays a role in the life of some creature. In the midafternoon heat, a bee fly was hovering near a delicate, daisylike erigeron. But it might only have been pausing in its search for another flower that is closely connected with its life cycle—and for the bee from which it gets its name. The Newberry penstemon, or mountain pride, has a wide mouth that gives easy entrance to any roving bee—or bee fly. In gathering pollen, the bee may attract the attention of the bee fly, a predator that sneaks up on its prey in a manner that circumvents the bee's barbed defenses. It does not attack directly; what it is likely to do is follow the bee and lay its eggs near the hive. The larvae from the fly then proceed to eat young bees as well as stored honey and pollen. The larvae invade the closed-off cells of the bee's nest, where they eventually become adult insects whose only purpose is to find another bee's nest and begin the process once more.

Before we encountered the bee fly a thunderhead had been building be-

LOOKING DOWNSTREAM AT STORM CLOUDS BUILDING IN McGEE CANYON

A CREEKSIDE PATTERN: RAINDROPS AND SEDGE

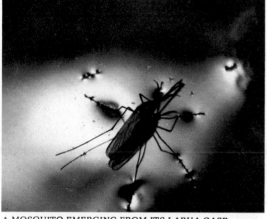

A MOSQUITO EMERGING FROM ITS LARVA CASE

A YELLOW-LEGGED FROG AWAITING A MEAL

AFTER THE STORM: SUNLIGHT ON GLACIAL POLISH NEAR LOWER McGEE LAKE

hind the heights ahead of us. Now rain came in on the westerly wind with stormy rumblings close behind. The rain, running across the rocks of the creek basin, gleamed with a contrasting brilliance against the sheen of glacial polish on the surface of the granite.

The rain started with a rush. But after a few minutes, it settled to a fine, steady downpour that promised to last some time. We decided to wait out the rest of the storm under the inadequate cover of a stand of lodgepoles growing near the creek margin. I am certain that the plants and creatures, even the stream itself, were grateful for the rain. The mountain frogs, their legs flashing as they plopped in and out of the rain-spattered stream, seemed to leap with more verve than before the storm. However, I was not thankful. Every half-stagnant pool on the course of McGee Creek, from the summit down to the stream's junction with Evolution Creek, harbors its mosquito eggs. And as the rain eased, the mosquitoes seemed to start hatching in greater abundance, adding to my annoyance at being wet.

The earliest mosquitoes to emerge in the spring, called snow-pool mosquitoes, hatch out of meltwater as soon as the sun can raise the water and air temperature even one degree above freezing. The rest take their turn, hatching throughout the summer. As we watched, one of the current crop, a tiny threadlike pupa, wiggled to the surface of a puddle, then split open its flexible casing and flew off as a mature insect as soon

as the wind dried its wings and hardened its external skeleton.

At that point my curiosity about mosquitoes evaporated. They rose in such clouds that a bare neck or forehead became the instant feeding ground for a half dozen or more insects. I found little comfort in the fact that the female mosquito bites me only because she needs the protein from mammalian blood to nourish the eggs she carries. Much more agreeable to contemplate was an insect I saw making holes in something

A SAWFLY ABOUT TO DEPOSIT HER EGGS

besides me. A sawfly—a kind of wasp—had lit on a nearby penstemon, where, using the sawlike appendage in its rear end, it was busy puncturing the underside of a leaf and laying its own eggs in the cuts.

As the afternoon deepened, we approached the stream's upper reaches. Above the main meadow the creek basin narrowed into a little rocky valley with a rich, hanging bog on one side, established where water, seeping from rock, has allowed

moss to grow and build up a moist cover of soil. This bog was filled with red and yellow columbine, the multiple blossoms of elephant heads, gooseberry currant and glorious red splashes of paintbrush.

Late Afternoon—Dwarf Plants

In this upper altitude, as we climbed along the last cascade toward the source lakes, the plants and insects were changing noticeably. The taller stream-bank willows were giving way to the tiny dwarf species, whose three- to four-inch height contains all the makings of a true tree with root system, trunk, branches, leaves and catkins.

Dwarf blueberry also appeared, and the lupines, whose stems farther downstream had been a foot long or more, now stood no more than six inches or so high. Back from the stream, the cold- and wind-resistant buckwheats crouched in tight bunches. And along the stem of one plant crawled a wingless crane fly, one of the several high-altitude insect species that through evolution have lost their wings; the mountain winds have too often made flight futile.

When we reached the summit lakes a setting sun had smeared a spectrum of pink and red and orange across the departing remnants of rain clouds. A few mountain sparrows still hopped about looking for insects, and an alpine chipmunk held its paws in an attitude of incongruous prayer as it munched its last meal before sundown. Soon bats would be out to gorge on the bonanza of mosquitoes.

A WINGLESS CRANE FLY

HUMMINGBIRD'S FAVORITE: PAINTBRUSH

A CLOSER LOOK: PAINTBRUSH AT DUSK

NEARING McGEE'S SOURCE

AN ALPINE CHIPMUNK EATING THE DAY'S LAST MEAL

We were now in the granite bowl beneath the ragged metamorphic masses of Mount Huxley and Mount McGee, where the creek has its beginnings in a chain of 10 lakes that lie at altitudes between 10,800 and 11,000 feet. The sides of the bowl are spotted with mattings of whitebark pine, smeared with lichen where moisture slides thinly over the rock and laced by cataracts of meltwater from crescents of lingering snow. Scoops of gray-black rubble tumble down the summit wall of Mount McGee. These are glacial moraines, half a dozen of them, none now holding a living glacier but some with lakelets of their own and each a reminder of the force of ice that carved the McGee Basin.

Dusk—at the Source

The lakes themselves are the clearest water, a pale glass green, melted out of the snowpack. As can be seen from the air, or on a map, they are arranged in a rough circle like a chaplet; the three largest are connected by inlet streams to a string of smaller ponds, lying up-slope to the southwest, that are the ultimate source of the creek. The lakes are rich in chemical nutrients, probably because each sits in its own small cup of rock where the full runoff from the surrounding land can collect in it. The movement of water within the lakes is slow, so the minute plant algae and insect larvae in them tend to take hold and grow, multiplying and adding their own fecundity to the water.

Since the lakes are shallow the sun can warm them during the brief summer, stimulating organic growth and giving off relatively warm water to McGee Creek as it emerges as a cat-

aract tumbling from the last lake.

As the time approached to make camp for the night, we came upon one final act in the round of life that turns near these mountain waters. It was the blossom of a shooting star, crimson pink with purple edges. As dusk fell, a pair of ants were

A SHOOTING STAR AT LAKESIDE

starting up its lower stem, evidently to capture the aphids that were nestled down within the blossom, their hip glands full of sweet nectar. By morning, we guessed, the ants would have carried the aphids down into an underground pen, to be kept and tended for their nectar. In the morning, we looked; ants and aphids were gone. The flower remained.

THE SOURCE: LOWER McGEE LAKE

5/ The Cabinet of Curiosities

...At last they looked from their prison over drifted walls of dazzling white, that towered twenty feet above their heads. BRET HARTE/ *THE OUTCASTS OF POKER FLAT*

The month is April. Spring is in the valleys below the Sierra, and along the eastern scarp the snow is melting up the mountainsides in a ragged line of rotting drifts. In the timbered canyons the ground is bare to 7,000 feet, and on the rock faces of the scarp above Owens Valley the snow line has backed up all the way to the crest, leaving only tendrils of white reaching down the flanks wherever there is a gully's shade or a northerly exposure. But beyond that crest in the high world of the Sierra heartland, winter's cold hand has not relaxed its grip, and much of the land retains an arctic look. West of Mount Whitney, where three of us have been living above 10,000 feet for the better part of a week, the meadows lie beneath sweeps of snow, frozen hard in the morning though melted by the midday sun into sharp, close-set corrugations. North for more than 180 miles the few roads across the mountains are closed as they have been since November, blocked by drifts. Within the great bowls where the mountains' contours trap the damp winds sweeping up from the Pacific, the snowpack remains 12 to 20 feet deep in places. Scattered glades of young hemlock on the forested western slope has been bowed and bent so deeply by the weight of snow that the trees lie supine, entirely covered beneath the drifts, where they will remain until the final melt releases them and, with a soft rush, they spring erect once more.

The high country seems to be clinging to a final moment of rest under

the diminishing white blanket. And the quiet pervading the wilderness suggests that only in winter is the Sierra truly wild and natural, as it once was. "The thing that saves this country is the winter," a fisherman had said last fall. "For nine months a year it lies under snow and has an opportunity to rejuvenate itself, to restore itself. If the wilderness got the kind of use for 12 months that it gets for a couple of months in summer, there'd be nothing left."

At the moment we seem to be the only intruders upon an enormous stretch of alpine landscape, and we have a serene feeling that plenty is left of the wilderness, especially that most precious commodity—solitude. True, some 200 miles north thousands of skiers are crawling over the slopes on the wilderness fringe at resorts like Squaw Valley, Sugar Bowl, Alpine Meadows and Heavenly Valley, and closer by at Mammoth Mountain in the central Sierra. Yosemite, too, has its own modest ski area; and spotted along the snowed-over track of the Tioga Pass road perhaps half a dozen winter campers are roughing it with nylon tents and goose-down sleeping bags. But that is all. We came into the high country, two Sequoia National Park rangers and I, by helicopter some days ago, skimming over an 11,000-foot pass near Mount Whitney, to be dropped on the snow of Crabtree Meadow three miles southwest of the peak. Since then we have spent our days traveling overland on skis with our food and clothes and sleeping bags stuffed into 40-pound packs. Nights we have bedded down in back-country cabins maintained by the Park Service in cooperation with the California Department of Water Resources' snow-survey crews. The surveyors come here at monthly intervals in winter to gauge the water content of the snowpack, and to predict the amount of water likely to run off in the spring and eventually to accumulate in lowland reservoirs. This snow-survey work is critical to the well-being of California. Los Angeles and San Francisco get much of their drinking water from the run-off of Sierra snow, and farmers in the Central Valley look to the Sierra reservoirs and west-slope rivers for economic survival.

When we first flew in, though reveling in the absence of man, we felt a little deprived because of the apparent scarcity of wild creatures in the winter wilderness. Thoreau once said, "In winter, nature is a cabinet of curiosities, full of dried specimens, in their natural order and position." And indeed the snow on the Sierra meadows and passes, seen from a low-skimming helicopter, appeared bare of wildlife tracks—no coyote, deer or, in fact, any overt sign that animals were abroad or that the plants had begun to stir with the imminent onset of spring. The

deer left these elevations when the November blizzards pushed them down to their winter foraging grounds in the foothills and valleys. They went out quickly with the first storms, moving down the bare, wind-blown ridges and avoiding gullies where accumulating drifts might trap them into the agony of starvation—or a swifter death from the coyotes that follow the herd to pick off faltering strays.

Now in April the deer are luxuriating among the shrubs and green grasses of the newly warmed lowlands, and it is a bit lonely up here without them. For in this part of the wilderness, a national park in which all animals are protected from shooting, the deer during the summer season are both abundant and bold. From July through September hardly a day passes without half a dozen of them drifting past a given campground or standing to watch the passage of a packtrain, their large eyes soft and unafraid like those of the animals in Edward Hicks's painting *Peaceable Kingdom*. They will be back soon, moving into the high mountains as tender shoots sprout from the snowbrush behind the line of melting drifts. But for now, the kingdom is empty of them.

It is empty, too, of the summer scramble of golden-mantled ground squirrels and chipmunks. The ground squirrels are all sleeping below the earth in tunnels or in burrows lined with shredded bark. As they lie curled into fat doughnuts of fur, their bodily commitment to hibernation during its deepest period is so complete that, to judge by vital signs, they are barely alive. Their breathing has slowed down from a norm of about 200 respirations per minute to four, their heartbeats from 200-400 to perhaps five. Their body temperatures have sunk to near freezing, and for about six months they have had no interest whatever in the waking world. The chipmunks are somewhat more active, occasionally foraging abroad and then returning underground to drowse near piles of stored seeds upon which they nibble during their intermittent awakenings.

With no rodents yet at large, the predator birds—the golden eagles, red-tails and the smaller Cooper hawks—that cruise the timbered meadows from spring through fall are still downslope where the pickings at mealtimes are better just now. Even the fish seem to be keeping themselves scarce. The high lakes have remained frozen; and beneath the ice the trout, their metabolic rates slowed by cold, are nosing about lazily to feed on the plankton and midges that have survived the 32° to 39° submarine temperatures. Most of the streams, however, have broken loose from their overarching snow tunnels to move as dark meanderings

among banks of sugary masses of decomposing snow crystals. At the edge of Crabtree Meadow where the helicopter dropped us, Whitney Creek is live and full and clear, apparently as congenial a fish habitat as it ever is in summer. Yet whenever we visit the creek to fill our water buckets we note no golden trout either feeding or holding in the pools. Nor are there any fresh depressions in the stream-bottom gravel to indicate that the lengthening days and more intense sunlight of spring have yet triggered the breeding instinct and impelled the goldens to start digging out new spawning beds with their fins.

In fact the only vestige of wildlife visible when first we came into the wilderness was a sparse fluttering of the small birds that are willing to make do on the spartan diet offered by the winter Sierra. Some chickadees and a homely but hardy little creature called the rosy finch were busy pecking on the chilled pine nuts and dead refrigerated bugs that melt or blow out of snowbanks.

It seems surprising that these tiny birds, even though protected by layers of feathers, should be able to survive year round in the high Sierra. But the past days in the high country have brought us several other more fundamental surprises. Among them has been a realization that the high-country winter, though justly famed for the violence of its climactic storms, is often quite docile and unthreatening, and sometimes not much colder than the summer.

From the very first day of our trip the weather has been consistently mild, almost idyllic. Afternoon temperatures have been about 50°, too warm on these cloudless days for sweaters or even for the gloves that prevent blisters from the rubbing and chafing of the ski-pole straps. By evening the thermometer has dropped near freezing, but the air is so dry and still that we find ourselves comfortable in T-shirts whenever we go outside to fetch water, split wood or wax our skis. Even at the grim hour of 4:30 a.m., when we roll out to get moving before the night-frozen snow turns too mushy for easy ski travel, the temperature has never been colder than 22° above zero. Such balminess in the high mountains is an unaccustomed joy for all three of us. I am an Easterner who has frozen his face and fingers more than once in the biting cold of a Vermont ski slope, and my two companions are natives of Colorado and Montana where cattle can die frozen in a standing position during a blizzard at 50° below.

It is true that on this Sierra trip we have been lucky to hit the warm days of a dry, early spring. Nevertheless, entries in the logs kept in each snow-survey cabin confirm that gentle weather is not uncommon

in the high country: "clear and warm," "clear and sunny today," "six-eight inches new snow, very little wind," "sunny in the morning." An account by an early snow surveyor named Orland Bartholomew of an odyssey he made in the winter of 1928-1929, beginning on Christmas near Mount Whitney and ending April 3 in Yosemite Park, has such comments as these: "No temperature below zero was recorded above 11,000 feet during the entire winter. . . . Many streams were found flowing almost unobstructed by ice or snow, even above 10,500 feet. The minimum temperature [January 10] on the summit of Mount Whitney at midevening was 26 degrees F." Even John Charles Frémont, that redoubtable chronicler of toil and hardship, revealed in his journals that the winter weather during his 1844 crossing of the Sierra was not always bad: "The purity and deep-blue color of the sky," he wrote, "are singularly beautiful; the days are sunny and bright, and even warm in the noon hours."

As with the weather, so with snow depths. They turned out to be nothing like the extremes I had expected. On this point, however, the old journals as well as some of the more modern accounts are superficially misleading, for they dwell on the most awesome of the Sierra winters. A diary of 1850 signed "Alice" tells of a three-week blizzard that left drifts 50 feet deep. In the winter of 1867 a village at Meadow Lake in the northern Sierra was buried so completely that the only way people could move from house to house was through snow tunnels dug across the main street. Eighty-five years later at Yuba Gap the crack streamlined train *City of San Francisco* stalled in snowdrifts and marooned 200 passengers for 96 hours before an escape path could be cut through to them. And in the winter of 1969 a world-record 11 feet of snow came down on Big Whitney Meadow in one 48-hour period in February. Even the conservative snow-survey logs for that year record heavy falls all over the high country: "Feb. 14 . . . Cabin was completely buried under 14-16 feet of snow. It took over an hour and a half of digging in a snowstorm to enter. Stovepipe was clogged. . . ."

It is true that at various times these sudden extremes of weather have made the Sierra a lethal place for anyone who allowed himself to be caught in the wrong place at the wrong time. The ill-advised and poorly equipped Donner party of 1846-1847 tried to start across the mountains too late in the season and foundered, tragically, in the drifts of an abnormally early and heavy snow year. In 1867 avalanches killed 20 men working on the Sierra link of the transcontinental railroad; and

A stand of stately white firs bears the weight of a heavy springtime snowfall in the middle elevations of Sequoia National Park.

in the 1960s more than a dozen skiers and climbers were swept away or died of exposure when they dared the wrong mountain at the wrong time. Perhaps the worst hazard of all is the wind, which can blow at cruel velocities. Summit-country gales have screamed at a recorded 120 miles per hour and more, whipping the snow with such ferocity that in one cabin a room was one quarter filled overnight by snow forced through the only aperture—a keyhole.

Such winds can kill a man or even a wild creature, not only by sheer force but by producing a climatic equivalent of cold called chill factor, which pulls effective temperatures down to arctic levels. For example, on a day when the thermometer reads 20°, a 25-mile-per-hour wind will create a climatic equivalent—i.e., chill factor—of 15° below zero; and on a rare zero day with 35-mile-per-hour winds the chill factor will be minus 52°. This chill factor, together with the long season of subfreezing nights and the sporadic occurrence of severe snows, accounts in large measure not only for the arctic appearance of the high country but also for the arctic adaptation of so many of its plants and animals.

Thus, the threat of deep winter pervades and controls all life. Yet now in April, normally the time of greatest snow accumulation before the major spring runoff, the placid look of the high Sierra indicates that massive snow depths—like low temperatures—are really the exception. The meteorological record confirms this impression, both as to frequency and locale. The Sierra enclaves such as Mammoth Mountain and the Donner Summit area, which regularly report depths of 25 feet, are at comparative low points in the crestline, where the Pacific air can slide through and dump its snow load. But above the 9,000-foot line, as in the region we are traveling west of Whitney, precipitation drops off and the average snow depth on April 1 for the southern Sierra is a modest 5 to 6 feet. And two winters out of three the snowpack is below average. This dry, warm year the snow measures only about two feet, with many of the south-facing slopes baked completely bare and the wind-blown summits as barren brown now as in October.

The other surprise for us in the high Sierra winter has come through a gradual understanding that the wilderness, though far emptier than in summer, is not really so dead as first impressions suggested—or as Thoreau implied. In fact the wild country has offered us excerpts from some fascinating stories as we have skied and climbed cross-country, keeping a close eye on the surface of the snow, on the trees and on the streams. Heading off from the Crabtree ranger cabin we saw the tracks,

A light snowfall freshens the wintry landscape framing Wolverton Creek in Sequoia National Park. The new snow is melting even before it stops falling, a sure sign that the mountain spring is just around the corner.

frozen in the snow and perhaps a week old, of a white-tailed jack rabbit that had run up the south bank of a stream in a pattern of light measured bounds. This lanky high-altitude creature, whose fluid gait is nothing like the comic bobbing of a garden rabbit, is able to stay alive and healthy at this season in the high country by nibbling on tree bark or dried grasses. Few four-footed animals venture higher or have made an easier adjustment to austere surroundings. During his 1929 journey, Bartholomew saw several of them sitting about on the bare windy summit of 14,042-foot Mount Langley.

Near the jack rabbit tracks on a patch of open ground we found a series of little meandering dirt piles that looked something like the tunnel roofings left on a lawn by moles. These were made by pocket gophers, chunky brown burrowers with long foreclaws and buckteeth for excavating. When the snow covers the ground, the pocket gophers tunnel into the drifts just above earth level. These snow tunnels are used as storage spaces for the dirt that the gopher continues to excavate from his deep earth tunnels all during the winter. He packs the loose dirt from his digs as tightly as possible into the snow tunnels, making a series of dirt corings in the snow. When the spring snowmelt starts, the corings sink to the ground surface and lie there in the twisting, elongated mounds that caught our eye.

A few yards beyond these corings was the first set of fresh tracks we had come upon. A mountain coyote had come down a draw at a dead run —probably within the past two days. His tracks appeared again and again as we climbed. There were no other tracks of any kind on the line of his run, indicating that he was not on a hunt when he went by. Privately I hoped he would be drawn tonight by the cooking smells from our cabin, because I love the sound of his cry and I wanted very much to hear him call to us from high on some nearby ridge.

In a high valley not far from Whitney Creek, at a steep place between two trees spaced about four yards apart, we came upon pairs of paw marks the size of a child's hand denting the snow in spacings of perhaps a foot. The prints were old and melted down though the contours of the pads still showed dimly. Our first guess was wolverine, but that was probably wrong since the wolverine, a surly carnivore who demands enormous amounts of both food and solitude, is perhaps the Sierra's scarcest and surely its most unsociable creature. More likely it was a pine marten, an agile arboreal weasel who likes to travel and hunt through the trees. One of his favorite foods is the chickaree, or

Douglas squirrel, which sees no need to hibernate during the winter. And though we ourselves have seen no such squirrels, the marten's tracks in the forest indicate that there are some around.

It is also possible that the marten was prowling for Sierra grouse. If so he was gambling on a very elusive meal, albeit a sumptuous one. The grouse is a heavily feathered bird whose cast-iron digestive tract allows him to flourish through the winter on a diet of pine or fir needles. Being not only plump and juicy but also resident the year round in the high country, the grouse is much admired by predators. As a result he is at times a deeply cautious bird, about as easy to catch unawares as a Las Vegas blackjack dealer. If the pine marten manages to catch him, however, the resulting banquet will solve all the marten's nourishment problems for at least a week.

These are the kinds of stories that are written on the snow for anyone who takes time to read and interpret them. And it occurred to us as we studied the marten's tracks that they were perfect evidence of the relationship of all things in the wilderness to each other. The pine marten sits atop a pyramid of life that begins far out on the Pacific Ocean —that began, in fact, far back in time when these mountains first formed. The mineral-rich soil of crumbled granite in the back country provides a seedbed for the pines. The pines sink roots into that soil and are nourished by meltwater from the snowpack, born of clouds that formed over the Pacific. Once grown the pines provide seeds for the chickaree or needles for the Sierra grouse. And they, in turn, are the food that sustains the pine marten. Knowing all this, John Muir wrote, "When we try to pick out anything by itself, we find it hitched to everything else in the universe." This is as true in winter as at any other time—and thus I find the winter wilderness not a cabinet full of dried specimens, but a rich and peaceable kingdom of creatures and growing things, each meeting the daily hardships of cold weather in his own way, or simply sleeping until, with spring, the living is easier.

Spring in the High Country

Springtime comes late to the high Sierra. Advancing upslope slowly from the foothills, it seldom reaches the 8,000-foot threshold to the uplands before mid-May, and it is often delayed until early June by a severe winter. The first sure sign of its arrival is the sound of flowing water —trickling rivulets and splashing streams, created or swollen by melting snows. And then the still, cold mountains come quickly alive.

The thick snowpack is relatively fast to melt in the mountain meadows, where only brief morning fogs screen the warming sun. The spongy flatlands sop up the moisture and burst into bloom, their flowers unfurling in broad swatches of contrasting pigments: creamy corn lilies, lavender shooting stars, pink or red monkey flowers. Most pervasive of all Sierra blossoms, monkey flowers bloom in any wet place—seepages, bogs and stream banks—from the lowest to the highest elevations.

As the meadows dry out, mariposa lilies (page 152) unfold cup-shaped flowers of various colors, all of them irresistible to flies, butterflies and bees. The insects, including clouds of mosquitoes that have hatched in puddles and bogs, keep the Sierra birds busy from dawn until twilight, when swarms of bats emerge to take up the chase.

The lower meadows may have been abloom for weeks before the snow melts in the forests at altitudes between 7,000 and 10,000 feet. Here the floral display is less extensive but even more various. Of the Sierra's 1,400 kinds of flowering plants, the greatest number dwell in these wooded regions, among them such early-blooming exotics as the crimson snow plant (page 149).

At altitudes above 10,000 feet, on the rocky windswept slopes leading to the Sierran summits, flowers rarely bloom before mid-July, and their whole growing season—spring, summer and fall—is crammed into just two months. Of the species native to the upper heights, perhaps the most evanescent is a small phloxlike mountaintop perennial called the sky pilot (after the slang term for chaplain—i.e., someone who shows the way to heaven). The sky pilot blooms only between late July and early August, and its blue flowers, growing in low clumps, hold their bloom for scarcely more than a few days. The wonder is not that they fade and shrivel so soon, but that they manage to blossom again at the next late spring thaw.

Imprisoned in ice at an altitude of 11,500 feet, a spiky seed stalk of timothy grass awaits the liberating warmth of the spring sun. For plants high up in the Sierra, the end of winter is retarded by nightly freezes continuing well into July.

A patch of snow (above), melting slowly on a mountainside, erodes into miniature peaks and valleys. After a snowy winter, the thick pack may not melt off completely until mid-August.

Hibernation over, ladybird beetles (right) emerge glistening wet from rotten logs and rock crevices to sun themselves. After a few days, they fly to the lowlands to feed on aphids.

A fast-growing snow plant, one of the first to appear in the forests, pokes its scaly head through a mat of twigs and pine needles. Within a week or so, the fleshy stalk grows to a height of eight to 12 inches. Then its scales curl back, exposing about two dozen bell-shaped crimson flowers. The plant is reputedly poisonous, but the Indians used it as a remedy for toothache.

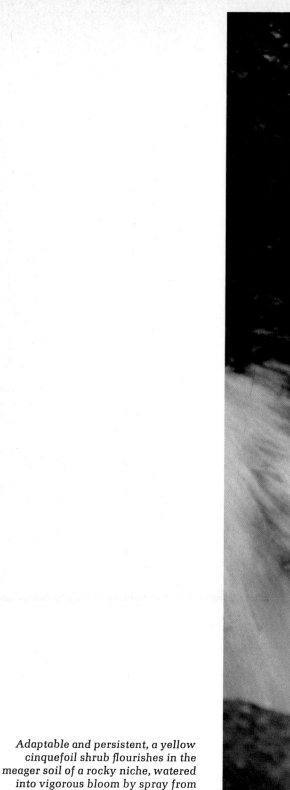

Adaptable and persistent, a yellow
cinquefoil shrub flourishes in the
meager soil of a rocky niche, watered
into vigorous bloom by spray from
melt-swollen waterfalls. The wind-
blown seeds of this perennial take root
almost anywhere they fall in the
middle altitudes. In the open meadows,
cinquefoil grows tall and coarse, but
on a windswept slope it becomes
a stunted, ground-hugging bush.

Far left: Springing up from the floor of a drying meadow, mariposa lilies put forth elegant blooms and long, arching, grasslike leaves. Most of their blossoms are creamy white, though rarer species produce flowers of yellow, red, lilac and purple. The bulbs from which the lilies grow were an important food for several Indian tribes. The Yosemites roasted and ate them gratefully as a gift from the gods.

Left: The tender sprout of a thistle breaks the raw earth shortly after the snow melts. The smooth pale shoot scarcely resembles the bristly mottled plant that soon develops from it.

Top right: A young mayfly basking on a rush branch whiles away its short life span as an adult. Myriads of mayfly larvae hatch in peaceful meadow pools, where most are gobbled up by rainbow trout. Those that survive to grow wings quickly breed a new generation, then sleep and die—within two days of the time when they were hatched.

Bottom right: A young Sierra newt lurks beneath a branch of manzanita, protecting its sensitive skin from the sun and concealing itself from prey and predator. The newts hatch in ponds and streams and spend their first winter under the ice as larvae. By spring they reach full growth (seven inches long) and develop legs and lungs for land travel. But they are seldom found very far from the water.

Blooming on an alpine slope 11,400 feet high near Elizabeth Pass in Sequoia National Park, paintbrush (left) and blue flax announce the coming of spring in mid-July. Both plants keep their blossoms through summer and fall, seasons crowded into seven or eight weeks; then they fade with the first hard frosts in the beginning of September.

6/ Preserving What Is Left

The real significance of wilderness is a cultural matter. It is far more than hunting, fishing, hiking, camping, or canoeing; it has to do with the human spirit.

SIGURD F. OLSON/ *THE SPIRITUAL ASPECTS OF WILDERNESS*

A hundred years after the first step to preserve wilderness was taken with the founding of Yosemite Park, one of the keepers of the high Sierra looked out upon the work of saving the wild land for the people and liked what he saw. In one year, seven million Americans had come bustling around the fringes of the back country. Two million of those had gone into the real wilderness to camp, to hike, to ride, to fish, to hunt, to cut timber, smoke marijuana, work mining claims, plan ski resorts, take pictures, play guitars, survey roads, set fires, make love, study rocks, admire animals, find peace, find themselves and, in my own case, to write a book. Statistical projections for the rest of the decade of the 1970s indicated, allowing for temporary drops in attendance, that every year there would be an average of 10 to 20 per cent more of us, each making his own best use of the wilderness that has been set aside for him. Most were aware, too, of the immeasurable value of the remaining parcel of wild countryside, at a time when the U.S. population was continuing to grow too fast, and when the appetite of an urbanized nation for the wilderness experience was growing still faster.

Happily, for the first time in many years there were signs that the Wilderness itself was larger. Nationally, despite groans from the mineral interests and pressure to cut more timber, Congress was moving ahead with its study of more than 55 million new acres that may be tucked under the protective umbrella of the Wilderness Act of 1964. In the Si-

erra alone the size of the legal Wilderness would almost double when 1.4 million acres of back country national park land, all part of the study, went into the official Wilderness Act category. This was a distinct and welcome change from the historic trend of a wilderness being steadily whittled down by a nation of hard-driving businessmen who have not yet shaken the frontier notion of every man's right to grab for himself one more piece of America. But as the new decade got under way, it was clear that big-league commercial land-grabbers were no longer a predominant threat, at least not in the Sierra where the land is now protected both by law and by vigilante groups of wilderness lovers standing on battle alert against any alleged marauder. For example:

□ When Walt Disney Productions got an agreement with the Sequoia National Forest to build a $35 million ski and summer resort in a wilderness enclave called Mineral King Valley, including a multilane access road through part of Sequoia National Park, the Sierra Club dragged the Disney people all the way to the U.S. Supreme Court in a concerted attempt to kill the project. Even if the Disney resort goes through, it may well be the last ski area built in the high country. At least one Sierra forest official has said firmly, "I don't think we'll be issuing any more ski-area permits around here."

□ Though a handful of gold and tungsten miners still scratched away at a few parts of the Sierra, empowered by a clause in the act permitting prospecting up to 1984, the filing of fresh claims had dwindled all through the region. And there was a fair chance that the public might ask Congress to shut down all mining in areas set aside by the Wilderness Act when the permissive clause expires.

□ Rangers long ago chased cattlemen and sheepherders from the parks, and from all but a few patches of national Wilderness. In a couple of places the ban on such livestock extends beyond the boundaries defined by the Wilderness Act to adjacent buffer areas of national forest where available forage has been set aside for deer and bighorn.

□ High-country lumbering was at a virtual standstill, forbidden in the parks and national Wilderness. In the outlying national forest, preservationist pressure had prodded Congress to hold hearings on the lumbering technique called clear-cutting, by which loggers hack whole areas clear of trees, leaving the land a gullied waste of stumps and shrubs and bulldozer tracks. "For the first time people are noticing the practices in forests near them," said a Congressional aide, "and they don't like what they see."

□ Even the highway builders, once encouraged by none other than John

Muir to build access routes for Sierra campers, were being cut off at the pass. When a trans-Sierra highway that would bisect the John Muir Trail near Mammoth Mountain was proposed, no less than 10 preservationist organizations came down against it.

Thus the state of the Sierra wilderness is indeed better. Much of the improvement came from the local Forest Service's own unmistakable expansion of policy beyond profit-oriented development of natural resources into preservation-oriented protection of the natural environment. This shift in emphasis by the Forest Service was part of a new and greater national concern with the quality of life in general, and the health of the wilderness in particular. "I think this new concern with the environment is heaven-sent," said one park superintendent. "It's the best thing that's ever happened to the wilderness—as long as it hasn't come too damned late." By the early 1970s there was scattered evidence throughout the Sierra wilderness that despite measures already taken and for reasons that very few people have been able to foresee, the hour might indeed be growing late. Yet largely because of the new environmental awareness, for every new problem faced by the wilderness, its protectors now seemed ready to apply remedies.

The troubles were plainly visible. The main trail from Echo Lake leading to Desolation Wilderness, like so many other back-country arteries, had come to look worn and pounded, and too much modified by the managing hand of man. The trail starts between a folksy village store and a boat-launching ramp at the edge of a parking lot, then climbs through a series of steps made from creosoted railroad ties set athwart the path. At intervals Forest Service signs say PUBLIC DOCK ¼ MILE or BOY SCOUT CAMP 300 YARDS. On Echo Lake a plastic speedboat cuts the surface into outflowing chevrons while shuttling as a water taxi between the parking lot and the Wilderness boundary near the lake's head. Cabins dot the shore, each one built on land leased to summer vacationers by the Forest Service.

From time to time the region reveals vestiges of true wilderness: a hawk flying close overhead with a chipmunk in its circled talons or the voice of the high country in the boughs of a red fir. Nevertheless, this gateway to Desolation Wilderness is distinctly man's country. There is none of the feeling of Inyo, the Dwelling Place of a Great Spirit. Desolation is, in fact, a mini-Wilderness, only 15 miles long by six to eight across. The mountains are smaller, softer of mien; the passes lie well below 10,000 feet, and they issue onto land more gentle and inviting

than the austere and sometimes forbidding high country to the south. "Desolation Wilderness is too pretty, too nice," says the young ranger who tends it; "and," he adds somewhat ruefully, "too available."

Because it is so available and so pretty and so small, it has become a kind of back-country pressure cooker wherein the residual problems affecting the whole Sierra wilderness have boiled up into a concentrated and sometimes unhappy stew. Here, as elsewhere in the Sierra, there are simply too many wilderness lovers for the existing terrain to absorb. And even the acquisition of new wilderness land will not wholly alleviate the situation. During the 1970 season, 106,000 people, about 44 per cent more than the preceding year, came into Desolation and very nearly loved the place to death. One day at the height of that summer, the young ranger looked down from a ridge onto Lake of the Woods where backpackers' tents were jammed together ridgepole to ridgepole, almost like a Civil War encampment. "This is not wilderness," he said. "This is not what Congress intended."

Nor was the scene on a similar day in the Minarets Wilderness along the shores of Shadow Lake, where no fewer than 450 people had set up their tents, built campfires, and were flailing the small body of water to a froth with their fly lines and spinning outfits. Nor, for that matter, was the seasonal circus at the summit of Mount Whitney itself, tallest peak in the Sierra Nevada and as such the physical climax of the greatest wilderness in the old continental United States. On an average summer weekend 300 people clamber to Whitney's top, clad in everything from bathing suits to business suits: a natty California hiker actually arrived in a Madison Avenue outfit complete with bow tie and fedora, carrying his duffel in a suitcase. On another occasion an unidentified pioneer battled to the top with a wheelbarrow. Over one recent Labor Day, 1,500 souls appeared on Whitney's crest, creating such a crush that the rangers cranked up the world's most exotic garbage vehicle, a helicopter, to land on the summit and evacuate the considerable mess the crowd had made.

There is a reasonable doubt that, in passing the Wilderness Act, Congress intended this sort of thing either.

Even in the fall, long after the crowds have gone, too much of the high country retains a frayed and weary look. The John Muir Trail itself, spine of the Sierra wilderness system, is scraped and pounded by horseshoes and hikers' boots into a dusty trough that in places has sunk two feet below the bordering meadow grass. And on a quiet autumn day at nearby Lake of the Woods, a horseman, dismounted and

Near twilight, a camper's tent stands anchored to a trail signpost (rear) on a gale-swept ridge high in the Sierra.

stretched out to rest by the shore, was harshly awakened by the snap of six rounds of light-caliber rifle fire, followed minutes later by the even booming of nine rounds from a heavier rifle. The sound was especially unsettling to this horseman since only a few years earlier, while topping a neighboring rise, he had heard the snick of a rifle bolt and found himself peering down the muzzle of a weapon held by a drunken deer hunter. "The big question," said the horseman to the ranger, "is how can we use the wilderness and still preserve it? Where a guy like Justice Douglas used to have the trails to himself, now they're covered with Joe Blow and a million Boy Scouts. But you can't close off the wilderness. That would defeat the purpose."

The ranger, being young, had a quick and contentious reply. "I don't manage people," he said. "I manage land. And if there is a conflict between land and people, the people have to go."

Hard words, and they are being backed by policy. Beginning with the 1971 season everyone who went into the Wilderness had to get a Forest Service permit on which he stated how many were in his party, how long they would stay and where they would enter and exit. "This is the first step in limiting visits," said the young ranger. "Initially the permits are to give us a count on the numbers of people that are going into the wilderness."

"But," said a supervisor of the John Muir Wilderness, "three to five years from now we'll be ready to use those permits to limit the numbers of visitors. There are two kinds of wilderness resources we have to protect: the actual physical resource and the more intangible solitude resource. Let's say you could have 100 people in a lake basin at a given time and not hurt the physical resource—but 100 people might hurt the solitude factor. So you'd take a lower figure. At a place like Shadow Lake it might be 20. And if someone got there, say, the second week in August and there were already 20 people on the lake, then he'd have to go somewhere else. A lot of people aren't going to like this, but I think we have the challenge of tailoring people's use to the carrying capacity of the land."

In certain parts of the Sierra back country, most particularly in the north-central portion of Kings Canyon and Sequoia National Parks, the rangers have already done some drastic tailoring. These parks recommend a maximum travel group of 25 (the Forest Service has done the same in its Wilderness); by 1973 the suggested party limit will become a hard and fast rule, and very soon after that the limit will drop still

lower. In addition there will be restrictions on the total number of people allowed in a given area of the wilderness at one time. Throughout the Charlotte and Rae Lakes district of Kings Canyon Park, no one may camp within 125 feet of any stream or lake, or stay more than one night at any given campsite. "This way," explains a ranger, "you don't get those big groups staying forever at one place and making a horrible mess. And by moving 'em back from the water, we cut down the danger of pollution and improve the esthetics. You know how sound carries over water; and you don't want to look across a lake and see 27 other tents on the opposite shore."

One back-country management report has gone so far as to recommend no washing or bathing in natural waterways: "Do you want to be taking a drink from some mountain brook," asks a backpacker, "and here comes the detergent from some guy's week-old socks and underwear floating by?" And since 1960 at the very popular camping area at Bullfrog Lake, where the trail ruts had begun to fork and crisscross like some bucolic freightyard and the tentsites were bare, trampled earth, all camping has been forbidden for an indefinite period to allow the land to restore itself.

The next obvious step, and one that seems to be coming to the Sierra —no matter how repulsive it is to a people raised in the free land tradition—is camping by advance reservation. "It can be handled fairly easily by computer, like Ticketron. I understand that some of the state parks are already doing it," says the young ranger at Desolation. "If, for example, there are two reservations for Lake Lucille next August 15, that's it. Nobody else can go."

"We know some people aren't going to like it," says another ranger, "but there is something we've all got to face. The time has passed when every American can go where he wants, stay as long as he wants, and do what he wants. If he keeps on, we won't have any wilderness left; and that's what we're being paid to preserve."

As an old-line wilderness lover, brought up in a nation created for the very purpose of encouraging every man to do his thing, I find the notions of restricted camping and computerized reservations revolting. And as a devout horseman I have some dark thoughts about the tight new grazing regulations. Yet I concur in both, absolutely. I would rather have my wilderness rationed than not have it at all. And if my horse hurts a meadow by grazing in it before the spring meltwater drains from the marshy areas, then my horse cannot go there, even if spring

does not end until August 1—as happens sometimes in the high country after a hard winter.

Thus I find myself in sullen agreement with the general drift of Park and Forest Service policy to keep us all from loving our wilderness to death. The fact is that the last real Sierra wilderness is already dead, in the sense that there is no surviving virgin spot where no man has ever been and where anyone who comes can be completely free. Nor has there been for many years.

Fortunately there are still quite a few places off the beaten track where the land, though visited before, still fits the words of the Wilderness Act: "retaining its primeval character and influence [and having] outstanding opportunities for solitude." I know of such places, but I am not going to tell you where they are, because then you would come to them and intrude upon my solitude. For the way of mankind is perverse and gregarious. He has legislated Wilderness because in his heart and bones he knows he needs it. But once he enters the wild country he seeks the company of others, bunching up at the better-known campgrounds and hiking only on the main trails.

For such reasons, the Wilderness unfortunately requires a fair degree of management by its custodians, and a high degree of restraint upon the part of its visitors. Both are necessary, for while the outlook for wilderness was never better, and the old, exploitative enemies of the wild country have been battled to a halt, most of us have failed to take note of the rise of the ultimate enemy to the sanctity of the Sierra. As Walt Kelly's comic-strip possum Pogo once said in a flash of brilliantly illuminated confusion, "We have met the enemy and he is us."

Of course no one, and particularly no member of the Sierra Club or any other such passionate organization, wants to think of himself as the worst enemy the wilderness ever had. But potentially he is and certainly together we all are, so long as we continue to go wherever we want, stay as long as we want and insist on doing whatever we want. Fortunately, most people are beginning to understand and to adjust to the concept of managed wilderness. Though they may concede the necessity of some of the things the wilderness custodians are doing to keep us lovers decently at bay (e.g., party limits, camping reservations), they remain confused about or ill-disposed toward some of the others. One is manipulation of the fish population. I happen to go into the wilderness for solitude and, incidentally, to fish. But, says a Forest Service administrator, "part of our problem is that a lot of people are coming here *just* to fish. And they don't care if they're in wilderness; they

carry out their quota of fish just the same. So maybe we're going to have to limit fish planting."

"It gets down to this," said one Fish and Game man, "and the decision goes way beyond just fishing into the whole question of wilderness use: do we want to have the real Wilderness that Congress legislated, where we manage for solitude and try to maintain a natural state of things? Or do we encourage things like fish planting to provide a recreational experience for masses of people?"

The question of hunting is just as difficult. Says one forest supervisor, "*Overnight* I'd like to eliminate firearms from the wilderness in summer." So would every single ranger and honest sportsman in the Sierra. Guns are scary to a lot of people; besides, there is no excuse for using them on songbirds, squirrels or marmots. But legitimate hunting for designated game animals in season is a far different story. For while it is pleasant to think theoretically of the wilderness as a sanctuary for all Numunana's creatures, more than a century of hunting has reshuffled the relationships of the Sierra's animals to one another. Many of the predators have been killed off. Without them, populations of the more benign herb-eating animals such as deer tend to expand to unhealthy dimensions. In the parks, where hunting has always been prohibited, rangers in small areas of the country near park boundaries quietly shoot dozens of mule deer from swollen herds that have overrun the available browse. To keep the herds down all over the wilderness, supervised hunters—perhaps with designated permits rather than unlimited licenses—could shoot this surplus.

Conflict springs from other kinds of wilderness use, creating nagging questions of safety and convenience that the wilderness managers are struggling to solve—or at least cope with. The most dramatic is the problem of keeping mountain climbers from killing themselves and risking the lives of large teams of volunteer rescuers. On a warm May morning not long ago five men clad in light pants and thin jackets started up Mount Ritter in the Minarets Wilderness. By midafternoon a blizzard had closed down on them, with winds of 60 to 70 miles per hour; next day four of the five were dead of exposure while some two dozen hikers and helicopter-borne rescuers scoured the mountains for the lone survivor. "The Sierra is very unforgiving," said a ranger, "if you don't respect its hazards."

Some of the Sierra's custodians are unforgiving too, and with reason. For 27 days one recent fall, two widely publicized rock climbers ham-

mered and clawed their way up the sheer southeast face of El Capitan in Yosemite as a rescue team of 18 other mountaineers waited to find out whether they would have to put their own necks on the line should the adventurers fail to reach the summit safely (they eventually made it). "Why the hell didn't they just climb the Empire State Building?" asked one veteran ranger who, like most other officials, saw the climb not as derring-do but a tiresome ego exercise that cost the Park Service a lot of time and worry, and could have cost lives as well. "If people go into the back country to climb or take other risks," he continued, "don't rescue them. They should be able to get themselves out."

Danger, and the willingness of each person to deal with it, are legitimate parts of the wilderness experience. But at the same time, everyone, including that hard-nosed official, privately concedes you cannot leave a trapped climber to rot on the end of his rope or tell an imprudent hiker's family you don't care that he froze to death. Thus normal rescue operations will continue in the wilderness, just as they do on public beaches. However, for high-risk adventures such as the El Capitan climb, it is perfectly reasonable, as several rangers have urged, to require mountaineers to bring their own backup rescue teams or otherwise satisfy the local wilderness authority that they have the experience and equipment for the ascent they are attempting.

On other, less spectacular aspects of wilderness administration the logic of evolving policies, however virtuous their intent, remains muddled. For example, the Congressional act specifies "the imprint of man's work [shall be] substantially unnoticeable." Yet the Forest Service continues to install such semicivilized amenities as latrines in the wilderness—"not as a convenience but to protect the ecology," as one ranger rationalized it.

Both the forest and park officials are still building and maintaining quite elaborate bridges over certain dangerous streams because they would prefer not to be fishing out the drowned bodies of wilderness purists who thought they had found a safe place to cross.

On the other hand they have taken several other measures so pure that even some purists are complaining. No fresh trails will be built anywhere in the wilderness; and trail maintenance will cease in the highest reaches of small segments within the very wildest places. Henceforth backpackers must restrict their travel to designated routes in such specified enclaves as the bighorn habitat, where their scampering on and off the trails was a serious disturbance to the animals. Existing trails, however logical and convenient, are being rerouted away from meadows so

The parallel gashes marring this alpine meadow were caused not by a four-wheeled vehicle but by horses' hoofs and hikers' feet. The meadows here are fragile because of the short summer at these altitudes. The soil remains moist and the grasses never root deeply. When animals and hikers keep trudging the same trail, they form a rut that is then deepened, often beyond repair, by frequent summer showers.

the fragile sod can recover. And the Forest Service plans to bar horses from limited areas in which the more exhaustive trail maintenance required for livestock passage is uncalled for. One of the better examples might be Desolation, a Wilderness so small that taking a horse there really cannot be justified.

The managers responsible for making and enforcing rules like this do so with one eye cocked on practical matters and the other scanning the wording of the laws that created their jobs. The conscientious effort this takes deserves credit. But paradoxically, hard, earnest work along such lines, carried out over a period of years, can create dilemmas never imagined either by legislators or managers. There is one problem, for instance, that the National Park Service has just barely begun to resolve: Is a park a natural museum or a national resort? When Congress first established the park system it laid down a mandate for the Service "to conserve the scenery and the natural . . . objects and the wild life therein and to provide for the enjoyment of the same in such manner and by such means as will leave them unimpaired for the enjoyment of future generations." Since then park personnel have generally been more zealous about providing for public enjoyment of the scenery and natural objects, and about conserving everything in sight, than they have been about leaving the place unimpaired. As a result large areas in the parks, especially in Yosemite and parts of Kings Canyon and Sequoia, became unhappy hybrids, something between low-class resorts and glorified zoos.

Yosemite, for example, has two hotels (with wire fences to keep deer out of the flower gardens), four swimming pools, five grocery and general stores, five souvenir shops, two golf courses, six gas stations, a bank, a hospital handling a brisk turnover of traffic casualties, regulated campsites on the valley floor for 6,000 people, an elaborate dude stable affiliated with a string of wooden-floored campsites for another 2,400 people and a vast motel complex that does a thriving trade with business conventioneers when not otherwise crowded to the eaves with ordinary tourists.

On a big holiday weekend up to 55,000 souls jam into the valley, trailing candy wrappers and carbon monoxide gas. And at such times, with excursionists tumbling out of buses and motorcyclists blasting around, some loaded with mescaline and malice, the park rangers exchange their Smokey Bear hats for plastic-visored riot helmets. Yosemite can take on the air of an extravagant Hollywood aberration, as if D. W. Griffith had created the setting and had then left the rest to a mad director

with a cast of all the wrong thousands. A dismal nadir occurred over one recent Fourth of July weekend, when a mounted troop of 16 rangers, augmented by a foot patrol of 21, charged a meadow full of stoked-up, bongo-drumming young people. The result was the first riot in national park history. Wielding lassoes, clubs, handcuffs and Mace, the rangers arrested 186 and left a rotten taste in everyone's mouths, including their own. The legacy of that unhappy day was that the image of park ranger changed temporarily from earnest custodian of the forest to "tree pig"—the coinage of one furious youngster—and the image of Yosemite to Woodstock West. Nobody was more aware of the change, or more dismayed than the rangers themselves, one of whom resigned outright while others commented grimly that they hadn't joined the park rangers to be policemen.

Fortunately both for present images and the future security of the whole park, the Service has already taken several giant steps toward cutting down both the congestion and the confusion in the valley—and eventually toward getting Yosemite out of the resort business altogether. Beginning around the time of the riot, automobiles and all other private vehicles were permanently barred from the east end of the valley, and the road system recast into a series of one-way loops that tended to make the frustrated car owner wish he had left his vehicle at home. And that was precisely the point. "The most jarring thing in Yosemite has been the cars," says the man directly responsible for valley administration. "After all, you're not allowed to drive your car through the Smithsonian," adds a ranger. Gradually, Yosemite is substituting public open-air shuttle buses for private automobiles with remarkably positive results.

As early as the autumn after the riot, the vacant parking lots in the east end were covered with carpets of pine needles, disturbed only by occasional strollers. The following July, though the visitor count for the month had increased from the riot year, most people left their cars in the remaining parking lots to walk around the valley. As a crowd they seemed much quieter and more attuned to the real beauty of Yosemite, and the valley itself seemed to be recapturing a sense of peace that it had lost too long ago. "It was so quiet," said one weekend visitor, "I thought maybe this was the way it was before people came to Yosemite." Better still, the park people had prepared a perceptive, tough-minded master plan for Yosemite's future use. The critical clauses in the plan spell out three aims: "The number of visitors [to] be controlled

in accordance with the Park's carrying capacity"; "prohibit the use of [all] automobiles for access and circulation, and . . . remove from the valley all service and concession activities not directly associated with or necessary to the valley's management and use."

To make the plan really succeed, however, the Park Service has to complete another giant step, this one away from its old habit of preserving natural things at the expense of natural processes. For years the service saw its parks as an aggregate of things—trees, deer and the like. And protection of these things became almost an obsession. No tree could burn, even if the threatening fire came from a source as natural as lightning. In fact the obsession became so complete that for a time it appeared no tree, however old, would even be permitted to fall: one survey recommended attaching guy wires to a huge sequoia nicknamed the Grizzly Giant to prevent it from toppling over, as nature clearly intended it would one day.

As a result of being protected from the natural processes out of which it had evolved, the character of the park wilderness began to change. Lodgepole pines invaded many of the meadows, which had been swept clean by periodic fires before the coming of the white man, and thick stands of fire-sensitive white fir and incense cedar began to crowd in on the great sequoias, filling up the open spaces their tiny seeds need in order to germinate.

"This kind of fire protection has been a doomsday route," said a ranger. "By eliminating any fire you change the composition of the forest. You get what we've got here now, which is a building of underbrush and fuel that could set off a real wildfire." The parks are beginning to correct this dangerous and basically unreal situation through selective clearing, and by the deliberate setting of controlled, small-radius fires that allow the proper balance of forest growth to regenerate. After that, natural fires can reassert the logic of their own control.

At the same time the managers of the parks are taking a continued hard look at their tendency to overprotect such creatures as deer, and at their way of introducing other soft-eyed forest denizens simply for the sake of having them around. Several years ago a colony of beaver, previously alien to the high Sierra, was planted in parts of the Kern River region in Sequoia Park. "Gosh, you couldn't say enough good about the beaver—we thought," sighed one ranger. "Cute, nature's little engineers, all that. But then they started cutting down all the trees and damming streams, deteriorating the golden trout habitat so the fish

couldn't spawn. And now we're faced with the job of taking out the beaver, killing them off. We really screwed up there."

"I think you've got to figure," said another, "that any ecosystem has developed over hundreds of thousands of years; and through evolution there is a balance between animals and vegetation. And once we break the glass, we have a lot of trouble putting the pieces back together. If we wipe out the grizzly or the condor, we can't really put them back —not the native animals, anyway. We've made some awful mistakes. And after a while it gets to be a zoo kind of thing, putting animals in there that don't belong."

Managing the animals that do belong can get to be a "zoo thing" that tampers with natural processes, and that tendency is being questioned, too. For in a park, as in any wilderness, it is a contradiction in terms for a visitor to be able to go to Point A with a guarantee of seeing a deer, or to Point B for a pine marten. Rather, such an encounter should be a chance one, as it has always been in nature. You should go into the wilderness simply to be there. And if you are very lucky, you may see a pine marten. And then, if you care, you can learn about him and his ways, how he relates to the land and the climate and they to him. And the next time you see him or read or hear of his like, the experience will be a deeper one. And you yourself will feel more at one with the pine marten, for that is what you are—simply another creature who is a significant and yet insignificant part of the land and the air, the soil and the climate, the animals and the forest. And then, perhaps for the first time in your life, you may truly begin to know something about yourself and your world. And that is what the wilderness is all about.

Discovery of a Living Valley

PHOTOGRAPHS BY HARALD SUND

Most visitors to Yosemite see the valley as a spectacle—huge in scale, full of brilliant light, dominated by towering rocks and leaping waterfalls. This is the awe-inspiring Yosemite, often described as timeless and enduring, a monument to the age of the glaciers. Hidden within it, visible to only a few, is another Yosemite, mysterious, vital, constantly changing, all unaware of the monumental role ascribed to it by men.

This is the Yosemite that intrigued photographer Harald Sund and became the subject of the pictures on the following pages. To discover it, Sund, who had never been there before, immersed himself in Yosemite, studying the details of the valley as well as its entirety, observing it by moonlight as well as in full sun. "Actually," he says, "I photographed the valley in my mind. Then I came back with the camera."

For Sund, the shot of El Capitan's granite flank (opposite), with the chip of rock in the foreground, brings the scale of the valley down to manageable proportion by contrasting the detail with the vast sweep of rock in the background. In making the picture of dewdrops sparkling on the grass of Leidig Meadow (pages 174-175), he was trying to offset the restful quality of the meadow's flat, green surface against the vertical harshness of the surrounding cliffs. The strange nighttime softness of Lower Yosemite Falls (page 176) dramatizes Sund's feeling of wonder that the water —seemingly so pliant—could carve the unyielding rock.

Inevitably, Sund could not transfer all of his perceptions onto film. He had to forgo a splendid shot of lightning striking Half Dome when his own position, on the tip of Glacier Point, became a storm target. A rare lunar rainbow, caused by moonlight on spray from a waterfall, eluded him when his camera proved unequal to the task of catching the spectral colors.

Generally, however, Sund managed to record things that the average visitor seldom sees: sunlight piercing the leaves of a dogwood grove ("The eye resists looking directly into the sun, but the camera doesn't flinch"), clouds shadowed by other clouds, the thrust of a tree root against a boulder. To Sund, all these speak of mysteries awaiting discovery, of a valley still in flux, an unfinished product. Far from being a memorial to the geological past, Sund's Yosemite is very much alive.

CATHEDRAL SPIRES FROM THE BASE OF EL CAPITAN AT 1 P.M.

GRANITE AND OAK: LEIDIG MEADOW AT 7:30 A.M.

BRIDALVEIL FALL, 5:30 A.M.

SUNRISE OVER HALF DOME FROM LEIDIG MEADOW AT 7:30 A.M.

LOWER YOSEMITE FALLS AT NIGHTFALL, 9 P.M.

SUNRISE ON THE MERCED RIVER, 7 A.M.

CLARK RANGE AND HALF DOME FROM GLACIER POINT, 8:30 P.M.

Acknowledgments

The author and editors of *The High Sierra* wish to thank the following persons who helped in its preparation: Paul Bateman, U.S. Geological Survey; Harold H. Biswell, Professor of Forestry, University of California, Berkeley; Gordon Boyd, Sequoia and Kings Canyon National Parks; B. K. Cooperrider, U.S. Forest Service; David J. Dunaway, Inyo National Forest; Dan Farris, Mammoth Lakes, Calif.; Coyt H. Hackett, Yosemite National Park; Bryan Harry, Yosemite National Park; John Thomas Howell, Curator Emeritus, Department of Botany, California Academy of Sciences, San Francisco; William C. Jones, Three Rivers, Calif.; Bruce Kilgore, Sequoia and Kings Canyon National Parks; A. Starker Leopold, Professor of Zoology, University of California, Berkeley; Elizabeth McClintock, California Academy of Sciences, San Francisco; Ronald J. McCormick, Inyo National Forest; John McLaughlin, Superintendent, Sequoia and Kings Canyon National Parks; Woodrow W. Middlekauff, Professor of Entomology, University of California, Berkeley; Lawrence S. Nahm, Yosemite National Park; James M. Olsen, Eldorado National Forest; Philip Pister, California Department of Fish and Game; Leo Porterfield, Inyo National Forest; Douglas Powell, Berkeley, Calif.; Joseph T. Radel, Bishop, Calif.; James L. Reveal, Assistant Professor of Botany, University of Maryland; Richard Riegelhuth, Sequoia and Kings Canyon National Parks; Edwin C. Rockwell, Inyo National Forest; Genny Schumacher Smith, Palo Alto, Calif.; Arnold P. Snyder, Sierra National Forest; Edward C. Stone, Professor of Forestry, University of California, Berkeley; Jan Studebaker, Yosemite Park and Curry Company; Clyde Wahrhaftig, Professor of Geology, University of California, Berkeley; Joseph Wampler, Berkeley, Calif.; Robert S. Wood, Berkeley, Calif.

Bibliography

*Available in paperback
†Paperback only

Best, Gerald M., *Snowplow: Clearing Mountain Rails*. Howell-North, 1966.
Brewer, William H., *Up and Down California in 1860-1864*. University of California Press, 1966.
*Brown, Vinson, and Robert Livezey, *The Sierra Nevadan Wildlife Region*. Naturegraph Company, 1962.
*Dobie, J. Frank, *The Voice of the Coyote*. University of Nebraska Press, 1961.
*Farquhar, Francis P., *History of the Sierra Nevada*. University of California Press, 1969.
Johnston, Hank, *They Felled the Redwoods*. Trans-Anglo Books, 1966.
Johnston, Verna R., *Sierra Nevada*. Houghton Mifflin Company, 1970.
†Matthes, François E., *The Incomparable Valley*. University of California Press, 1970.
Matthews, William H., III, *A Guide to the National Parks: Vol. I, The Western Parks*. Natural History Press, 1968.
†Muir, John, *The Mountains of California*. Natural History Books, 1961.
†Muir, John, and Richard Kauffman, *Gentle Wilderness*. Sierra Club-Ballantine Books, 1968.
*Munz, Philip A., *California Mountain Wildflowers*. University of California Press, 1969.
*Nash, Roderick, *Wilderness and the American Mind*. Yale University Press, 1967.
Roth, Hal, *Pathway in the Sky: The Story of the John Muir Trail*. Howell-North, 1965.
*Russell, Carl P., *100 Years in Yosemite*. Yosemite Natural History Assn., 1968.
†Schumacher, Genny, ed., *Deepest Valley*. Wilderness Press, 1969.
†Schumacher, Genny, ed., *The Mammoth Lakes Sierra*. Wilderness Press, 1969.
†Schwenke, Karl, and Thomas Winnett, *Sierra North*. Wilderness Press, 1967.
†Schwenke, Karl, and Thomas Winnett, *Sierra South*. Wilderness Press, 1968.
†Starr, Walter A., Jr., *Starr's Guide: Guide to the John Muir Trail and the High Sierra Region*. Sierra Club, 1970.
*Storer, Tracy I., and Robert L. Usinger, *Sierra Nevada Natural History*. University of California Press, 1968.

Picture Credits

Sources for pictures in this book are shown below. Credits for pictures from left to right are separated by commas, from top to bottom by dashes.

COVER–Jack H. Lawrence. Front end papers 1, 2–Harald Sund. End paper 3, page 1–Martin Litton. 2, 3–John O. Beahrs. 4, 5–Don Carlson. 6, 7–Jack H. Lawrence. 8, 9–David Muench. 10, 11–Harald Sund. 12, 13–Sonja Bullaty. 18-19–Map by R. R. Donnelley Cartographic Services.

CHAPTER 1: 23–David Muench. 35–From *John of the Mountains* by Linnie Marsh Wolfe, 1938, Houghton Mifflin Co., Boston. 36–Courtesy of the Bancroft Library. 37–Robert A. Weinstein.

38, 39–Courtesy of the Bancroft Library. 40, 41–Harold G. Schutt courtesy Tulare County Historical Society. 42, 43–Collection Roy D. Graves courtesy Gerald M. Best. 44–National Park Service. 45–Courtesy History Archives, Los Angeles County Museum of Natural History. 46, 47–Joseph Le Conte courtesy Sierra Club.

CHAPTER 2: 50, 51–W. C. Mendenhall courtesy U.S. Geological Survey. 54, 55–Frank Lerner. 65–Harald Sund. 66, 67–Sonja Bullaty. 68, 69, 70–David Muench. 71–Philip Hyde.

CHAPTER 3: 81–David Muench. 84–Angelo Lomeo. 85–Richard C. Burns except top left Sonja Bullaty. 89 through 103–Sonja Bullaty and Angelo Lomeo.

CHAPTER 4: 107, 108–Kenneth W. Fink. 112–Ronn Patterson–Tom Tracy from PhotoFind, Ed Park. 113–Ronn Patterson. 115–Hal Roth. 116, 117–Kenneth W. Fink, Maurice G. Hornocker. 120–David J. Dunaway. 124–Map by Margo Dryden. 125 through 135–David Cavagnaro.

CHAPTER 5: 140, 141, 143–Sonja Bullaty. 147–George Silk for LIFE magazine. 148, 149–George Silk for LIFE magazine except center Edward S. Ross. 150, 151–George Silk for LIFE magazine. 152, 153–David Cavagnaro except bottom right Tom Myers. 154, 155–Sonja Bullaty.

CHAPTER 6: 160–George Silk for LIFE magazine. 165–Sue Rayfield. 171 through 179–Harald Sund.

Index